*The Heritage
of Literature
Series*

SECTION A NO. 5

LIGHTER ESSAYS

THE HERITAGE OF LITERATURE SERIES

General Editor: E. W. PARKER, M.C.

A series that will lead to wider horizons by awakening a love of good books, and by providing a key to the treasures of the world's best thought

TRAVEL AND ADVENTURE

ESSAYS AND BELLES LETTRES

DRAMA

FICTION

MYTHS AND FOLK LORE

HISTORY

LIFE AND LETTERS

POETRY

———

" TARYE NO LENGER; TOWARD THYN HERITAGE HAST ON THY WEYE."
—JOHN LYDGATE.

ROBERT LYND

LIGHTER ESSAYS

SELECTED AND EDITED

BY

A. J. MERSON, M.A.
Headmaster, Carrick Academy, Maybole

With a Frontispiece

LONGMANS, GREEN AND CO.

LONDON . NEW YORK . TORONTO

LONGMANS, GREEN AND CO. LTD.
39 PATERNOSTER ROW, LONDON, E.C.4
17 CHITTARANJAN AVENUE, CALCUTTA
NICOL ROAD, BOMBAY
36A MOUNT ROAD, MADRAS

LONGMANS, GREEN AND CO.
55 FIFTH AVENUE, NEW YORK
221 EAST 20TH STREET, CHICAGO
88 TREMONT STREET, BOSTON

LONGMANS, GREEN AND CO.
215 VICTORIA STREET, TORONTO

New Impression January 1941

PRINTED IN GREAT BRITAIN BY
NORTHUMBERLAND PRESS LIMITED
GATESHEAD ON TYNE

FOREWORD

THE word " Essay " was first used as a literary term by a Frenchman of the sixteenth century, Michel de Montaigne, who invented it to show that his compositions were " attempts " at a new form of literature. He drew up no rules for his own guidance nor did he pretend to exhaust any subject; he wrote in the manner and at the length that the mood of the moment dictated. Hence his essays are coloured by his own personality, and it was this expression of personality that was to remain the chief characteristic and the peculiar charm of the essay.

As Montaigne showed, there is no limit to the subjects of which the essayist may write. " Everything I see or hear," says Alexander Smith, the author of *Dreamthorp*, " is an essay in bud. The world is everywhere whispering essays." But no matter what the subject is, the cat by the fire, a pig in its sty, a visit to relations in the country, or an encounter with gipsies, the writer casts it in the mould of his own mind and it becomes just as much a part of him as the expression on his features or the tone of his voice. If therefore you would appreciate any essay to the full, search for the man behind the essay —the urbane Addison, the lovable, whimsical Lamb, the genial Mr. Lynd.

ACKNOWLEDGMENTS

For permission to include copyright matter I am indebted to the following:

" Alpha of the Plough " and Messrs. J. M. Dent & Sons Ltd., for the essays " In Praise of Walking," from *Pebbles on the Shore*, and " February Days," from *Windfalls*; Mr. W. N. P. Barbellion and Messrs. Chatto & Windus, for " An Autumn Stroll," from *Enjoying Life*; Mr. Edmund Blunden and Messrs. Longmans, Green & Co. Ltd., for " The Hop Leaf," from *The Face of England*; Sir James Frazer and Messrs. Macmillan & Co. Ltd., for " The Spectator in the Country," from Sir James Frazer's *The Gorgon's Head*; Mr. W. H. Hudson and Messrs. J. M. Dent & Sons Ltd., for the extract " My Friend the Pig," from *The Book of a Naturalist*; Mr. Robert Lynd, for his essay "Londoners," from *Solomon in All His Glory*; Mr. Lloyd Osbourne and Messrs. Charles Scribner's Sons, for the passage " The Trials of a Donkey-Driver," from R. L. Stevenson's *Travels with a Donkey*; and Mr. F. Wood Jones and Messrs. Edward Arnold & Co., for the essay entitled " The Sea-Serpent," from Mr. Wood Jones's *Unscientific Essays*.

The Frontispiece, a drawing of Robert Lynd, by Corbluth, after a camera-portrait by Howard Coster.

CONTENTS

CONTENTS

IN PRAISE OF WALKING

I STARTED out the other day from Keswick with a ruck-sack on my back, a Baddeley in my pocket, and a companion by my side. I like a companion when I go a-walking. "Give me a companion by the way," said Sterne, "if it be only to remark how the shadows lengthen as the sun declines." That is about enough. You do not want a talkative person. Walking is an occupation in itself. You may give yourself up to chatter at the beginning, but when you are warmed to the job you are disposed to silence, drop perhaps one behind the other, and reserve your talk for the inn table and the after-supper pipe. An occasional joke, an occasional stave of song, a necessary consultation over the map—that is enough for the way.

At the head of the Lake we got in a boat and rowed across Derwentwater to the tiny bay at the foot of Cat-bells. There we landed, shouldered our burdens, and set out over the mountains and the passes, and for a week we enjoyed the richest solitude this country can offer. We followed no cut-and-dried programme. I love to draw up programmes for a walking tour, but I love still better to break them. For one of the joys of walking is the sense of freedom it gives you. You are tied to no

time-table, the slave of no road, the tributary of no man.
If you like the road you follow it; if you choose the pass
that is yours also; if your fancy (and your wind) is for
the mountain tops, then over Great Gable and Scawfell,
Robinson and Helvellyn be your way. Every short cut
is for you, and every track is the path of adventure.
The stream that tumbles down the mountain side is your
wine cup. You kneel on the boulders, bend your head,
and take such draughts as only the healthy thirst of the
mountains can give. And then, on your way again
singing:

> Bed in the bush with the stars to see,
> Bread I dip in the river—
> There's the life for a man like me,
> There's the life for ever.

What liberty is there like this? You have cut your
moorings from the world, you are far from telegraphs
and newspapers and all the frenzies of the life you have
left behind you, you are alone with the lonely hills and
the wide sky and the elemental things that have been
from the beginning and will outlast all the tortured
drama of men. The very sounds of life—the whistle of
the curlew, the bleating of the mountain sheep—add to
the sense of primeval solitude. To these sounds the
crags have echoed for a thousand and ten thousand
years; to these sounds and to the rushing of the winds
and the waters they will echo ten thousand years hence.
It is as though you have passed out of time into eternity,
where a thousand years are as one day. There is no
calendar for this dateless world. The buzzard that you

have startled from its pool in the gully and that circles round with wide-flapping wings has a lineage as ancient as the hills, and the vision of the pikes of Langdale that bursts on you as you reach the summit of Esk hause is the same vision that burst on the first savage who adventured into these wild fastnesses of the mountains.

And then as the sun begins to slope to the west you remember that, if you are among immortal things, you are only a mortal yourself, that you are getting footsore, and that you need a night's lodging and the comforts of an inn. Whither shall we turn? The valleys call us on every side. Newlands wide vale we can reach, or cheerful Borrowdale, or lonely Ennerdale, or—yes, to-night we will sup at Wastdale, at the jolly old inn that Auld Will Ritson used to keep, that inn sacred to the cragsman, where on New Year's Eve the gay company of climbers foregather from their brave deeds on the mountains and talk of hand-holds and foot-holds and sing the song of " The rope, the rope," and join in the chorus as the landlord trolls out:

> I'm not a climber, not a climber,
>   Not a climber now,
> My weight is going fourteen stone—
>   I'm not a climber now.

We shall not find Gaspard there to-night—Gaspard, the gay and intrepid guide from the Dauphiné, beloved of all who know the lonely inn at Wastdale. He is away on the battle-field fighting a sterner foe than the rocks and precipices of Great Gable and Scawfell. But Old Joe, the shepherd, will be there—Old Joe, who has never been in a train or seen a town, and whose special glory is that he can pull uglier faces than any man in Cumberland. He will not pull them for anybody—only when he is in a good humour and for his cronies in the back parlour. To-night, perchance, we shall see his eyes roll as he roars out the chorus of " D'ye ken John Peel? " Yes, Wastdale shall be to-night's halt. And so over Black Sail, and down the rough mountain-side to the inn whose white-washed walls hail us from afar out of the gathering shadows of the valley.

To-morrow? Well, to-morrow shall be as to-day. We will shoulder our rucksacks early, and be early on the mountains, for the first maxim in going a journey is the early start. Have the whip-hand of the day, and then you may loiter as you choose. If it is hot, you may bathe in the chill waters of those tarns that lie bare to the eye of heaven in the hollows of the hills— tarns with names of beauty and waters of such crystal purity as Killarney knows not. And at night we will come through the clouds down the wild course of Rosset Ghyll and sup and sleep in the hotel hard by Dungeon Ghyll, or, perchance, having the day well in hand, we will push on by Blea Tarn and Yewdale to Coniston, or by Easedale Tarn to Grasmere, and so to the Swan at the foot of Dunmail Raise. For we must call at the Swan. Was it not the Swan that Wordsworth's " Waggoner " so triumphantly passed? Was it not the Swan to which Sir Walter Scott used to go for his beer when he was staying with Wordsworth at Rydal Water? And behind the Swan is there not that fold in the hills where Wordsworth's " Michael " built, or tried to build, his sheepfold? Yes, we will stay at the Swan whatever befalls.

16

And so the jolly days go by, some wet, some fine, some a mixture of both, but all delightful, and we forget the day of the week, know no news except the changes in the weather and the track over the mountains, meet none of our kind except a rare vagabond like ourselves —with rope across his shoulder if he is a rock-man, with rucksack on back if he is a tourist—and with no goal save some far-off valley inn where we shall renew our strength and where the morrow's uprising to deeds shall be sweet.

I started to write in praise of walking, and I find I have written in praise of Lakeland. But indeed the two chants of praise are a single harmony, for I have written in vain if I have not shown that the way to see the most exquisite cabinet of beauties in this land is by the humble path of the pedestrian. He who rides through Lakeland knows nothing of its secrets, has tasted of none of its magic.

" ALPHA OF THE PLOUGH "—*Pebbles on the Shore.*

AN AUTUMN STROLL

On a recent day in early autumn I stood leaning against a tall larch tree, on the edge of a broad plantation, in a woodland corner of the North of Devon. I had been an indoor prisoner for a long, long time, and this was a first country walk. What a blessing to breathe again the sweet, honey-scented air! How fresh-looking those meadows below, how green the trees! For, autumn notwithstanding, the herbage had just reached that stage when it crowds all its many-tinted greens and the whole of its remaining vitality into one last sunny day; then very quickly follow death and decay.

Even now, a few leaves on that sturdy oak, solitary in the field yonder, have turned to golden russet; the larches, too, overhead are growing ragged and thin, and as the leaves begin to fall a few hardy cones that have weathered one winter already peep from their summer bowers and prepare once more for the blasts. Just in front, over the hedge of thick blackthorn, a furze brake —or, as Devonshire folk would say, "vuzz" brake— spreads its tangled meshes, and I hear the rabbits rustling and scuttling among the bushes as though out for a general romp; up from the valley on the left comes the rushing sound of running water, and, far ahead, the plain is lost to view in a medley of converging hills. Plump on the horizon appear the heath-clad downs, their glowing purple clear and luscious as the bloom on a peach.

In the solemnity and silence of the fir-wood I find an analogy with the atmosphere of mysterious repose in some stately cathedral, in the midst of, yet apart from, the vortex of busy life without. Into the dim recesses of the fir-wood few sounds of natural life make their way —except, perhaps, the call of a crow passing over the tree-tops, or the scream of a startled jay; and these are but momentary. Presently I leave the still woods to pass through the gap in the hedge, and so enter the busy whirl of wild life in the fields. It is a long way down to the little ivy-covered bridge that spans the river, so I do not hurry.

Here the delicate eyebright grows so thickly that I cannot help but crush it as I walk. Clusters of red bartsia and musk mallows crowd out the green of a grassy bank. Near a tangle of bramble and sweet briar the knapweed rears its head of pink flowerets.

A few steps further on, with inquisitive intent, I over-turn a large flat stone (flat stones always harbour something interesting). Under this one is a nest of black ants. Away they run, carrying their eggs into the heart of the nest; but—yes, I thought so, right in the centre of the principal doorway, lolls the ugly, repulsive form of a devil's coach-horse, or, as he is sometimes called, the Rove beetle. The busy ants find him distinctly in the way, and so they energetically set to work to shift the obstruction. Two climb on to his head and vigor-ously gnaw the bases of his stout antennæ, and two others attack the front pair of legs—a leg apiece! Another pinches the soft elongated abdomen. The effect on the beetle is ludicrous. He snaps his jaws like an angry terrier. Then he frantically waves his " yard-arms," and eventually, being nipped in many additional places by a reinforcement, he cocks his tail over his back and very reluctantly (for he has been most comfortably ensconced) beats a hasty retreat. This is a great victory for the ants, as the devil's coach-horse is a noted warrior in the insect world. With renewed energy the ants re-commence their labours, and when I re-pass the spot on my way home not an ant is to be seen, for the treasures have been successfully removed " downstairs." I carefully put the stone back in its place.

Here is the little bridge at last. It is built for the cattle to cross upon from one meadow to the other when the stream is flooded with winter rains. During the summer they scorn the bridge and splash across the water. Always a beautiful spot, it is never more beauti-ful than in the early autumn; moreover, for me it has pleasant associations. Up beyond the bridge is a water-fall, over which the water gallops from the shimmering, silvery weir-pool above into the boulder-scattered shallows beneath. Solitude adds to the charm. Indeed, a companion's voice could scarce be heard amidst the little thunder of these dancing " falls."

That huge holt held an otter once, but whether he is there now is doubtful. Anyway, if I would see him, I must be up betimes in the morning; I shall not see him to-day. A green canopy of hazels and alders smiles over all, and through the interstices the sun shines, dappling the shady waters with light. It was in this very stream, I recall, that I first made acquaintance with the wild red deer. This is how it was. The staghounds had met in the morning up at the village, and, according to custom, tufters were taken to a large wood some miles distant, which, for some unexplained reason, is always a favourite one with the deer. I had never yet seen a wild red deer, so I was anxious to make the best of my opportunities. No other horse but "Shanks' pony" was available, and those "in the know" told me that the best thing I could do, in the circumstances, was to walk to a certain bridge, as the deer, when roused, almost invariably came straight down the combe and entered an oak coppice, to the left of the high road and adjoining this very bridge. I took the advice, and saw something far prettier than the antlered stag, with the eager hounds in his wake. I had been waiting patiently for upwards of two hours on the bridge and was engrossed in watching a silent riverside tragedy—the capture of a water-vole by a greedy heron—when, treading softly round the bend of the stream, and advancing calmly and quietly and in the fearlessness of privacy and innocence, there swept across my vision the charmingest, dearest, prettiest little calf in creation. He was a tiny fellow with brown coat and shapely neck, slender legs, and hazel eyes. Upon his lordship's arrival, the heron dropped the struggling vole, and he lumbered away and pitched on a tall elm; a startled trout swam headlong downstream. The calf, small as he was, was making quite a commotion.

In the helter-skelter in the wood beyond, probably he and his mother had been separated, and for the first time in his life he had to think for himself, to act on his own initiative. The oft-repeated words of the hind his mother, that the water carries no scent, seemed now very valuable to him. He heard the waters calling:

> I carry no scent, come here, come here,
> For I am the friend of the wild red deer.

So down towards the bridge he came, where I saw him. But he did not catch sight of me for several minutes, although he seemed to scent me. He grew fussy and, half playfully, half nervously, browsed the leaves of a nut-tree. But he did not eat them—he disdainfully tossed them over his head, as an old stag would a turnip. In jerking his head aloft he suddenly saw me! For a moment he looked spellbound. He did not move, nor did I. We looked straight into each other's eyes. Then he blinked twice or thrice, and slowly came nearer! Had he passed below the bridge I could have touched him with my hand. But I was disappointed, for on moving my hand the slightest bit downwards the little creature (now standing right below me) pricked his ears, jumped lightly on to the bank and then trotted across the meadow into a copse, where I earnestly hope he remained undisturbed.

W. N. P. Barbellion—*Enjoying Life*.

THE ADVENTURES OF A SHILLING

I was last night visited by a friend of mine, who has an inexhaustible fund of discourse, and never fails to entertain his company with a variety of thoughts and hints that are altogether new and uncommon. Whether it were in complaisance to my way of living, or his real opinion, he advanced the following paradox, " That it required much greater talents to fill up and become a retired life, than a life of business." Upon this occasion he rallied very agreeably the busy men of the age, who only valued themselves for being in motion, and passing through a series of trifling and insignificant actions. In the heat of his discourse, seeing a piece of money lying on my table, " I defy (says he) any of these active persons to produce half the adventures that this twelvepenny piece has been engaged in, were it possible for him to give us an account of his life."

My friend's talk made so odd an impression upon my mind, that soon after I was a-bed I fell insensibly into a most unaccountable reverie, that had neither moral nor design in it, and cannot be so properly called a dream as a delirium.

Methought the shilling that lay upon the table reared

itself upon its edge, and turning the face towards me, opened its mouth, and in a soft silver sound, gave me the following account of his life and adventures:

"I was born (says he) on the side of a mountain, near a little village of Peru, and made a voyage to England in an ingot, under the convoy of Sir Francis Drake. I was, soon after my arrival, taken out of my Indian habit, refined, naturalized, and put into the British mode, with the face of Queen Elizabeth on one side, and the arms of the country on the other. Being thus equipped, I found in me a wonderful inclination to ramble, and visit all parts of the new world into which I was brought. The people very much favoured my natural disposition, and shifted me so fast from hand to hand, that before I was five years old, I had travelled into almost every corner of the nation. But in the beginning of my sixth year, to my unspeakable grief, I fell into the hands of a miserable old fellow, who clapped me into an iron chest, where I found five hundred more of my own quality who lay under the same confinement. The only relief we had was to be taken out and counted over in the fresh air every morning and evening. After an imprisonment of several years, we heard somebody knocking at our chest and breaking it open with a hammer. This we found was the old man's heir, who, as his father lay a-dying was so good as to come to our release: he separated us that very day. What was the fate of my companions I know not: as for myself, I was sent to the apothecary's shop for a pint of sack. The apothecary gave me to a herb-woman, the herb-woman to a butcher, the butcher to a brewer, and the brewer to his wife, who made a present of me to a nonconformist preacher. After this manner I made my way merrily through the world; for, as I told you before, we shillings love nothing so much as travelling. I sometimes fetched in a shoulder of mutton, sometimes a play-book, and often had the satisfaction to treat a Templar at a twelvepenny ordinary, or carry him, with three friends, to Westminster Hall.

" In the midst of this pleasant progress which I made from place to place, I was arrested by a superstitious old woman, who shut me up in a greasy purse, in pursuance of a foolish saying, " That while she kept a Queen Elizabeth's shilling about her, she should never be without money." I continued here a close prisoner for many months, till at last I was exchanged for eight and forty farthings.

" I thus rambled from pocket to pocket till the beginning of the civil wars, when, to my shame be it spoken, I was employed in raising soldiers against the king: for being of a very tempting breadth, a sergeant made use of me to inveigle country fellows, and list them in the service of the parliament.

" As soon as he had made one man sure, his way was to oblige him to take a shilling of a more homely figure, and then practise the same trick upon another. Thus I continued doing great mischief to the crown, till my officer, chancing one morning to walk abroad earlier than ordinary, sacrificed me to his pleasures, and made use of me to bestow me on a milk-maid. This wench bent me, and gave me to her sweetheart, applying more properly than she intended the usual form of, " To my love and from my love." This ungenerous gallant marrying her within a few days after, pawned me for a dram of brandy, and drinking me out next day, I was beaten flat with a hammer, and again set a-running.

"After many adventures, which would be tedious to relate, I was sent to a young spendthrift, in company with the will of his deceased father. The young fellow, who I found was very extravagant, gave great demonstrations of joy at the receiving of the will: but opening it, he found himself disinherited and cut off from the possession of a fair estate, by virtue of my being made a present to him. This put him into such a passion, that after having taken me in his hand, and cursed me, he squirred me away from him as far as he could fling me. I chanced to light in an unfrequented place under a dead wall, where I lay undiscovered and useless, during the usurpation of Oliver Cromwell.

"About a year after the king's return, a poor cavalier that was walking there about dinner-time, fortunately cast his eye upon me, and, to the great joy of us both, carried me to a cook's shop, where he dined upon me, and drank the king's health. When I came again into the world, I found that I had been happier in my retirement than I thought, having probably, by that means, escaped wearing a monstrous pair of breeches.

"Being now of great credit and antiquity, I was rather looked upon as a medal than an ordinary coin; for which reason a gamester laid hold of me, and converted me to a counter, having got together some dozens of us for that use. We led a melancholy life in his possession, being busy at those hours wherein current coin is at rest, and partaking the fate of our master, being in a few moments valued at a crown, a pound, or a sixpence, according to the situation in which the fortune of the cards placed us. I had at length the good luck to see my master break, by which means I was again sent abroad under my primitive denomination of a shilling.

"I shall pass over many other accidents of less moment, and hasten to that fatal catastrophe, when I fell into the hands of an artist, who conveyed me under ground, and with an unmerciful pair of shears, cut off my titles, clipped my brims, retrenched my shape, rubbed me to my inmost ring, and, in short, so spoiled and pillaged me, that he did not leave me worth a groat. You may think what a confusion I was in, to see myself thus curtailed and disfigured. I should have been ashamed to have shown my head, had not all my old acquaintance been reduced to the same shameful figure, excepting some few that were punched through the belly. In the midst of this general calamity, when everybody thought our misfortune irretrievable, and our case desperate, we were thrown into the furnace together, and (as it often happens with cities rising out of a fire) appeared with greater beauty and lustre than we could ever boast of before. What has happened to me since this change of sex which you now see, I shall take some other opportunity to relate. In the meantime, I shall only repeat two adventures, as being very extraordinary, and neither of them having ever happened to me above once in my life. The first was, my being in a poet's pocket, who was so taken with the brightness and novelty of my appearance, that it gave occasion to the finest burlesque poem in the British language, entitled from me, 'The Splendid Shilling.' The second adventure, which I must not omit, happened to me in the year 1703, when I was given away in charity to a blind man; but indeed this was by a mistake, the person who gave me having heedlessly thrown me into the hat among a pennyworth of farthings."

JOSEPH ADDISON—*The Tatler*.

THE TRIALS OF A DONKEY-DRIVER

THE bell of Monastier was just striking nine as I got quit of these preliminary troubles and descended the hill through the common. As long as I was within sight of the windows, a secret shame and the fear of some laughable defeat withheld me from tampering with Modestine. She tripped along upon her four small hoofs with a sober daintiness of gait; from time to time she shook her ears or her tail; and she looked so small under the bundle that my mind misgave me. We got across the ford without difficulty—there was no doubt about the matter, she was docility itself—and once on the other bank, where the road begins to mount through pine-woods, I took in my right hand the unhallowed staff, and with a quaking spirit applied it to the donkey. Modestine brisked up her pace for perhaps three steps, and then relapsed into her former minuet. Another application had the same effect, and so with the third. I am worthy the name of an Englishman, and it goes against my conscience to lay my hand rudely on a female. I desisted, and looked her all over from head to foot; the poor brute's knees were trembling and her breathing was distressed; it was plain that she could go no faster on a hill. God forbid, thought I, that I should brutalize this innocent creature; let her go at her own pace, and let me patiently follow.

What that pace was, there is no word mean enough to describe; it was something as much slower than a walk as a walk is slower than a run; it kept me hanging on each foot for an incredible length of time; in five minutes it exhausted the spirit and set up a fever in all the muscles of the leg. And yet I had to keep close at hand and measure my advance exactly upon hers; for if I dropped a few yards into the rear, or went on a few yards ahead, Modestine came instantly to a halt and began to browse. The thought that this was to last from here to Alais nearly broke my heart. Of all conceivable journeys, this promised to be the most tedious. I tried to tell myself it was a lovely day; I tried to charm my foreboding spirit with tobacco; but I had a vision ever present to me of the long, long roads, up hill and down dale, and a pair of figures ever infinitesimally moving, foot by foot, a yard to the minute, and, like things enchanted in a nightmare, approaching no nearer to the goal.

In the meantime there came up behind us a tall peasant, perhaps forty years of age, of an ironical snuffy countenance, and arrayed in the green tail-coat of the country. He overtook us hand over hand, and stopped to consider our pitiful advance.

" Your donkey," says he, " is very old? "

I told him, I believed not.

Then, he supposed, we had come far.

I told him we had but newly left Monastier.

" *Et vous marchez comme ça!* " cried he; and, throwing back his head, he laughed long and heartily. I watched him, half prepared to feel offended, until he had satisfied his mirth; and then, " You must have no pity on these animals," said he; and, plucking a switch out of a thicket, he began to lace Modestine about the stern-works, uttering a cry. The rogue pricked up her ears and broke into a good round pace, which she kept up without flagging, and without exhibiting the least symptom of distress, as long as the peasant kept beside us. Her former panting and shaking had been, I regret to say, a piece of comedy.

My *deus ex machina*, before he left me, supplied some excellent, if inhumane, advice; presented me with the switch, which he declared she would feel more tenderly than my cane; and finally taught me the true cry or masonic word of donkey-drivers, " Proot! " All the time, he regarded me with a comical, incredulous air, which was embarrassing to confront; and smiled over my donkey-driving, as I might have smiled over his orthography, or his green tail-coat. But it was not my turn for the moment.

I was proud of my new lore, and thought I had learned the art to perfection. And certainly Modestine did wonders for the rest of the forenoon, and I had a breathing space to look about me. It was Sabbath; the mountain-fields were all vacant in the sunshine; and as we came down through St. Martin de Frugères, the church was crowded to the door, there were people kneeling without upon the steps, and the sound of the priest's chanting came forth out of the dim interior. It gave me a home feeling on the spot; for I am a countryman of the Sabbath, so to speak, and all Sabbath observances, like a Scottish accent, strike in me mixed feelings, grateful and the reverse. It is only a traveller, hurrying by like a person from another planet, who can rightly enjoy the peace and beauty of the great ascetic feast. The sight of the resting country does his spirit good. There is something better than music in the wide unusual silence; and it disposes him to amiable thoughts, like the sound of a little river or the warmth of sunlight.

In this pleasant humour I came down the hill to where Goudet stands in a green end of a valley, with Château Beaufort opposite upon a rocky steep, and the stream, as clear as crystal, lying in a deep pool between them. Above and below, you may hear it wimpling over the stones, an amiable stripling of a river, which it seems absurd to call the Loire. On all sides Goudet is shut in by mountains; rocky footpaths, practicable at best for donkeys, join it to the outer world of France; and the men and women drink and swear, in their green corner or look up at the snow-clad peaks in winter from the threshold of their homes, in an isolation, you would think, like that of Homer's Cyclops. But it is not so the postman reaches Goudet with the letter-bag; the aspiring youth of Goudet are within a day's walk of the railway at Le Puy; and here in the inn you may find a engraved portrait of the host's nephew, Régis Sena, "Professor of Fencing and Champion of the two Americas," a distinction gained by him, along with the sum of five hundred dollars, at Tammany Hall, New York, on the 10th April, 1876.

I hurried over my midday meal, and was early forth again. But, alas, as we climbed the interminable hill upon the other side, "Proot!" seemed to have lost its virtue. I prooted like a lion, I prooted mellifluously like a sucking-dove; but Modestine would be neither softened nor intimidated. She held doggedly to her pace; nothing but a blow would move her, and that only for a second. I must follow at her heels, incessantly belabouring. A moment's pause in this ignoble toil and she relapsed into her own private gait. I think I never heard of anyone in as mean a situation. I must reach the lake of Bouchet, where I meant to camp, before sundown, and, to have even a hope of this, I must instantly maltreat this uncomplaining animal. The sound of my own blows sickened me. Once, when I looked at her, she had a faint resemblance to a lady of my acquaintance who formerly loaded me with kindness; and this increased my horror of my cruelty.

To make matters worse, we encountered another donkey, ranging at will upon the roadside; and this other donkey chanced to be a gentleman. He and Modestine met nickering for joy, and I had to separate the pair and beat down their young romance with a renewed and feverish bastinado. If the other donkey had had the heart of a male under his hide, he would have fallen upon me tooth and hoof; and this was a kind of consolation—he was plainly unworthy of Modestine's affection. But the incident saddened me, as did everything that spoke of my donkey's sex.

It was blazing hot up the valley, windless, with vehement sun upon my shoulders; and I had to labour so consistently with my stick that the sweat ran into my eyes. Every five minutes, too, the pack, the basket and the pilot-coat would take an ugly slew to one side or the other; and I had to stop Modestine, just when I had got her to a tolerable pace of about two miles an hour, to tug, push, shoulder and readjust the load. And at last, in the village of Ussel, saddle and all, the whole hypothec turned round and grovelled in the dust below the donkey's belly. She, none better pleased, incontinently drew up and seemed to smile; and a party of one man, two women and two children came up, and, standing round me in a half-circle, encouraged her by their example.

I had the devil's own trouble to get the thing righted; and the instant I had done so, without hesitation, it toppled and fell down upon the other side. Judge if I was hot! And yet not a hand was offered to assist me. The man, indeed, told me I ought to have a package of a different shape. I suggested, if he knew nothing better to the point in my predicament, he might hold his tongue. And the good-natured dog agreed with me smilingly. It was the most despicable fix. I must plainly content myself with the pack for Modestine, and take the following items for my own share of the portage: a cane, a quart flask, a pilot-jacket heavily weighted in the pockets, two pounds of black bread, and an open basket full of meats and bottles. I believe I may say I am not devoid of greatness of soul; for I did not recoil from this infamous burden. I disposed it, heaven knows how, so as to be mildly portable, and then proceeded to steer Modestine through the village. She tried, as was indeed her invariable habit, to enter every house and every courtyard in the whole length; and, encumbered as I was, without a hand to help myself, no words can render an idea of my difficulties. A priest, with six or seven others, was examining a church in process of repair, and he and his acolytes laughed loudly as they saw my plight. I remembered having laughed myself when I had seen good men struggling with adversity in the person of a jackass, and the recollection filled me with penitence. That was in my old light days, before this trouble came upon me. God knows at least that I shall never laugh again, thought I. But oh, what a cruel thing is a farce to those engaged in it!

A little out of the village, Modestine, filled with the demon, set her heart upon a by-road, and positively refused to leave it. I dropped all my bundles, and, I am ashamed to say, struck the poor sinner twice across the face. It was pitiful to see her lift up her head with shut eyes, as if waiting for another blow. I came very near crying; but I did a wiser thing than that, and sat squarely down by the roadside to consider my situation under the cheerful influence of tobacco and a nip of brandy. Modestine, in the meanwhile, munched some black bread with a contrite hypocritical air. It was plain that I must make a sacrifice to the gods of shipwreck. I threw away the empty bottle destined to carry milk; I threw away my own white bread, and, disdaining to act by general average, kept the black bread for Modestine; lastly, I threw away the cold leg of mutton and the egg-whisk, although this last was dear to my heart. Thus I found room for everything in the basket, and even stowed the boating-coat on the top. By means of an end of cord I slung it under one arm; and although the cord cut my shoulder, and the jacket hung almost to the ground, it was with a heart greatly lightened that I set forth again.

I had now an arm free to thrash Modestine, and cruelly I chastised her. If I were to reach the lakeside before dark, she must bestir her little shanks to some

35

tune. Already the sun had gone down into a windy looking mist; and although there were still a few streak of gold far off to the east on the hills and the black fir woods, all was cold and grey about our onward path An infinity of little country by-roads led hither and thither among the fields. It was the most pointles labyrinth. I could see my destination overhead, o rather the peak that dominates it; but choose as pleased, the roads always ended by turning away from it, and sneaking back towards the valley, or northwar along the margin of the hills. The failing light, th waning colour, the naked, unhomely, stony countr through which I was travelling, threw me into som despondency. I promise you, the stick was not idle; think every decent step that Modestine took must hav cost me at least two emphatic blows. There was no another sound in the neighbourhood but that of m unwearying bastinado.

Suddenly, in the midst of my toils, the load once mor bit the dust, and, as by enchantment, all the cords wer simultaneously loosened, and the road scattered with m dear possessions. The packing was to begin again from the beginning; and as I had to invent a new and bette system, I do not doubt but I lost half an hour. It bega to be dusk in earnest as I reached a wilderness of tur and stones. It had the air of being a road which shoul lead everywhere at the same time; and I was falling int something not unlike despair when I saw two figure stalking towards me over the stones. They walked on behind the other like tramps, but their pace was remark able. The son led the way, a tall, ill-made, sombre Scottish-looking man; the mother followed, all in he

Sunday's best, with an elegantly embroidered ribbon to her cap, and a new felt hat atop, and proffering, as she strode along with kilted petticoats, a string of obscene and blasphemous oaths.

I hailed the son, and asked him my direction. He pointed loosely west and north-west, muttered an inaudible comment, and, without slackening his pace for an instant, stalked on, as he was going, right athwart my path. The mother followed without so much as raising her head. I shouted and shouted after them, but they continued to scale the hillside, and turned a deaf ear to my outcries. At last, leaving Modestine by herself, I was constrained to run after them, hailing the while. They stopped as I drew near, the mother still cursing; and I could see she was a handsome, motherly, respectable-looking woman. The son once more answered me roughly and inaudibly, and was for setting out again. But this time I simply collared the mother, who was nearest me, and, apologizing for my violence, declared that I could not let them go until they had put me on my road. They were neither of them offended—rather mollified than otherwise; told me I had only to follow them; and then the mother asked me what I wanted by the lake at such an hour. I replied, in the Scottish manner, by inquiring if she had far to go herself. She told me, with another oath, that she had an hour and a half's road before her. And then, without salutation, the pair strode forward again up the hillside in the gathering dusk.

I returned for Modestine, pushed her briskly forward, and, after a sharp ascent of twenty minutes, reached the edge of a plateau. The view, looking back on my day's journey, was both wild and sad. Mount Mézenc and the peaks beyond St. Julien stood out in trenchant gloom against a cold glitter in the east; and the intervening field of hills had fallen together into one broad wash of shadow, except here and there the outline of a wooded sugar-loaf in black, here and there a white irregular patch to represent a cultivated farm; and here and there a blot where the Loire, the Gazeille, or the Laussonne wandered in a gorge.

Soon we were on a high-road, and surprise seized on my mind as I beheld a village of some magnitude close at hand; for I had been told that the neighbourhood of the lake was uninhabited except by trout. The road smoked in the twilight with children driving home cattle from the fields; and a pair of mounted stride-legged women, hat and cap and all, dashed past me at a hammering trot from the canton where they had been to church and market. I asked one of the children where I was. At Bouchet St. Nicolas, he told me. Thither, about a mile south of my destination, and on the other side of a respectable summit, had these confused roads and treacherous peasantry conducted me. My shoulder was cut, so that it hurt sharply; my arm ached like toothache from perpetual beating; I gave up the lake and my design to camp, and asked for the *auberge*.

R. L. Stevenson—*Travels with a Donkey.*

38

A COUNTRY CONGREGATION

I AM always very well pleased with a country Sunday, and think, if keeping holy the seventh day were only a human institution, it would be the best method that could have been thought of for the polishing and civilizing of mankind. It is certain the country people would soon degenerate into a kind of savages and barbarians, were there not such frequent returns of a stated time, in which the whole village meet together with their best faces, and in their cleanliest habits, to converse with one another upon indifferent subjects, hear their duties explained to them, and join together in adoration of the Supreme Being. Sunday clears away the rust of the whole week, not only as it refreshes in their minds the notions of religion, but as it puts both the sexes upon appearing in their most agreeable forms, and exerting all such qualities as are apt to give them a figure in the eye of the village. A country fellow distinguishes himself as much in the churchyard, as a citizen does upon the Change, the whole parish-politics being generally discussed in that place either after sermon or before the bell rings.

My friend Sir Roger, being a good churchman, has beautified the inside of his church with several texts of his own choosing. He has likewise given a handsome pulpit-cloth, and railed in the communion-table at his own expense. He has often told me, that at his coming to his estate he found his parishioners very irregular; and that in order to make them kneel and join in the responses, he gave every one of them a hassock and a common prayer book: and at the same time employed an itinerant singing-master, who goes about the country for that purpose, to instruct them rightly in the tunes of the psalms; upon which they now very much value themselves, and indeed outdo most of the country churches that I have ever heard.

As Sir Roger is landlord to the whole congregation, he keeps them in very good order, and will suffer nobody to sleep in it besides himself; for if by chance he has been surprised into a short nap at sermon, upon recovering out of it he stands up and looks about him, and if he sees anybody else nodding, either wakes them himself, or sends his servants to them. Several other of the old knight's particularities break out upon these occasions. Sometimes he will be lengthening out a verse in the singing psalms, half a minute after the rest of the congregation have done with it; sometimes when he is pleased with the matter of his devotion, he pronounces amen three or four times to the same prayer; and sometimes stands up, when everybody else is upon their knees, to count the congregation, or see if any of his tenants are missing.

I was yesterday very much surprised to hear my old friend, in the midst of the service, calling out to one John Matthews to mind what he was about, and not disturb the congregation. This John Matthews it seems

40

is remarkable for being an idle fellow, and at that time was kicking his heels for his diversion. This authority of the knight, though exerted in that old manner which accompanies him in all circumstances of life, has a very good effect upon the parish, who are not polite enough to see anything ridiculous in his behaviour; besides that the general good sense and worthiness of his character make his friends observe these little singularities as foils that rather set off than blemish his good qualities.

As soon as the sermon is finished, nobody presumes to stir till Sir Roger is gone out of the church. The knight walks down from his seat in the chancel between a double row of his tenants that stand bowing to him on each side: and every now and then inquires how such an one's wife, or mother, or son, or father do, whom he does not see at church; which is understood as a secret reprimand to the person that is absent.

The chaplain has often told me that upon a catechising-day, when Sir Roger has been pleased with a boy that answers well, he has ordered a bible to be given him next day for his encouragement; and sometimes accompanies it with a flitch of bacon to his mother. Sir Roger has likewise added five pounds a year to the clerk's place; and that he may encourage the young fellows to make themselves perfect in the church service, has promised upon the death of the present incumbent, who is very old, to bestow it according to merit.

The fair understanding between Sir Roger and his chaplain, and their mutual concurrence in doing good, is the more remarkable, because the very next village is famous for the differences and contentions that rise between the parson and the 'squire, who live in a

41

B*

perpetual state of war. The parson is always preaching at the 'squire; and the 'squire to be revenged on the parson never comes to church. The 'squire has made all his tenants atheists and tithe-stealers; while the parson instructs them every Sunday in the dignity of his order, and insinuates to them in almost every sermon that he is a better man than his patron. In short, matters are come to such an extremity, that the 'squire has not said his prayers either in public or private this half year; and that the parson threatens him, if he does not mend his manners, to pray for him in the face of the whole congregation.

Feuds of this nature, though too frequent in the country, are very fatal to the ordinary people; who are so used to be dazzled with riches, that they pay as much deference to the understanding of a man of an estate, as of a man of learning; and are very hardly brought to regard any truth, how important soever it may be, that is preached to them, when they know there are several men of five hundred a year who do not believe it.

JOSEPH ADDISON—*The Spectator.*

A PORTRAIT GALLERY

I was this morning walking in the gallery, when Sir Roger entered at the end opposite to me, and advancing towards me, said he was glad to meet me among his relations, the de Coverleys, and hoped I liked the conversation of so much good company, who were as silent as myself. I knew he alluded to the pictures, and as he is a gentleman who does not a little value himself upon his ancient descent, I expected he would give me some account of them. We were now arrived at the upper end of the gallery, when the knight faced towards one of the pictures, and as we stood before it, he entered into the matter, after his blunt way of saying things as they occur to his imagination, without regular introduction, or care to preserve the appearance of chain of thought.

" It is," said he, " worth while to consider the force of dress; and how the persons of one age differ from those of another, merely by that only. One may observe also, that the general fashion of one age has been followed by one particular set of people in another, and by them preserved from one generation to another. Thus the vast jetting coat and small bonnet, which was the habit in Henry the Seventh's time, is kept on in the yeoman

of the guard; not without a good and politic view
because they look a foot taller, and a foot and a hal'
broader: besides that the cap leaves the face expanded
and consequently more terrible, and fitter to stand a
the entrances of palaces.

" This predecessor of ours you see is dressed after thi
manner, and his cheeks would be no larger than min
were he in a hat as I am. He was the last man tha
won a prize in the Tilt-yard (which is now a commo
street before Whitehall). You see the broken lance tha
lies there by his right foot. He shivered that lance o
his adversary all to pieces; and bearing himself, loo
you, sir, in this manner, at the same time he cam
within the target of the gentleman who rode agains
him, and taking him with incredible force before hin
on the pommel of his saddle, he in that manner rid th
tournament over, with an air that showed he did i
rather to perform the rule of the lists than expose hi
enemy; however it appeared he knew how to make us
of a victory, and with a gentle trot he marched up to
gallery where their mistress sate (for they were rivals
and let him down with laudable courtesy and pardonab
insolence. I do not know, but it might be exactly wher
the coffee-house is now.

" You are to know this, my ancestor was not only o
a military genius, but fit also for the arts of peace, fo
he played on the bass-viol as well as any gentleman a
court; you see where his viol hangs by his basket-hi
sword. The action at the Tilt-yard you may be sur
won the fair lady, who was a maid of honour, and th
greatest beauty of her time; here she stands the ne
picture. You see, sir, my great-great-great-grandmothe

has on the new-fashioned petticoat, except that the modern is gathered at the waist; my grandmother appears as if she stood in a large drum, whereas the ladies now walk as if they were in a go-cart. For all this lady was bred at court, she became an excellent country-wife, she had ten children, and when I show you the library, you shall see in her own hand (allowing for the difference of the language) the best receipt now in England both for an hasty-pudding and a white-pot.

" If you please to fall back a little, because it is necessary to look at the three next pictures at one view; these are three sisters. She on the right hand, who is so very beautiful, died a maid; the next to her, still handsomer, had the same fate, against her will; this homely thing in the middle had both their portions added to her own, and was stolen by a neighbouring gentleman, a man of stratagem and resolution, for he poisoned three mastiffs to come at her, and knocked down two deer-stealers in carrying her off. Misfortunes happen in all families. The theft of this romp, and so much money, was no great matter to our estate. But the next heir that possessed it was this soft gentleman, whom you see there. Observe the small buttons, the little boots, the laces, the slashes about his clothes, and, above all, the posture he is drawn in (which to be sure was his own choosing); you see he sits with one hand on a desk writing and looking as it were another way, like an easy writer, or a sonneteer. He was one of those that had too much wit to know how to live in the world; he was a man of no justice, but great good manners; he ruined everybody that had anything to do with him, but never said a rude thing in his life; the most indolent person in the world he would sign a deed that passed away half his estate with his gloves on, but would not put on his hat before a lady if it were to save his country. He is said to be the first that made love by squeezing the hand. He left the estate with ten thousand pounds debt upon it; but, however, by all hands I have been informed that he was every way the finest gentleman in the world. That debt lay heavy on our house for one generation, but it was retrieved by a gift from the honest man you see there, a citizen of our name, but nothing at all akin to us. I know Sir Andrew Freeport has said behind my back, that this man was descended from one of the ten children of the maid-of-honour I showed you above; but it was never made out. We winked at the thing indeed, because money was wanting at that time."

Here I saw my friend a little embarrassed, and turned my face to the next portraiture.

Sir Roger went on with his account of the gallery in the following manner: " This man (pointing to him I looked at) I take to be the honour of our house—Sir Humphrey de Coverley; he was in his dealings as punctual as a tradesman, and as generous as a gentleman. He would have thought himself as much undone by breaking his word, as if it were to be followed by bankruptcy. He served his country as knight of this shire to his dying day. He found it no easy matter to maintain an integrity in his words and actions, even in things that regarded the offices which were incumbent upon him, in the care of his own affairs and relations of life, and therefore dreaded (though he had great talents) to go into employments of state, where he must be exposed to the snares of ambition. Innocence of life and great ability were the distinguishing parts of his character; the latter, he had often observed, had led to the destruction of the former, and he used frequently to lament that great and good had not the same signification. He was an excellent husbandman, but had resolved not to exceed such a degree of wealth; all above it he bestowed in secret bounties many years after the sum he aimed at for his own use was attained. Yet he did not slacken his industry, but to a decent old age spent the life and fortune which was superfluous to himself, in the service of his friends and neighbours."

Here we were called to dinner, and Sir Roger ended the discourse of this gentleman, by telling me, as we followed the servant, that this his ancestor was a brave man, and narrowly escaped being killed in the civil wars; " For," said he, " he was sent out of the field upon a private message the day before the battle of Worcester." The whim of narrowly escaping by having been within a day of danger, with other matters above mentioned, mixed with good sense, left me at a loss whether I was more delighted with my friend's wisdom or simplicity.

SIR RICHARD STEELE—*The Spectator.*

THE SPECTATOR IN THE COUNTRY

THE end of my visit to Sir Roger is now approaching, and I confess that I contemplate my return to town with a degree of regret which I certainly did not expect to feel when I left London for Coverley. In truth, I fall more and more in love with the country. The soft green of fields and meadows, of trees and hedges, the flowery lanes, the winding, willow-fringed streams, the prospect of far blue hills, the great expanse of sky, flecked with white summer clouds at noon or kindled into crimson and gold at sunset, the freshness and sweetness of the air, the peace and tranquillity poured like a healing balm over all—these things affect me with a pleasure which I feel deeply but am powerless to express. I begin to think of forswearing the city and retiring far from its smoke and uproar, its fever and fret, to spend the remainder of my days in some rural solitude. If ever I do so, I cannot imagine any spot that would attract me more than Coverley, and if Sir Roger would have me for a tenant, I should be content to take up my abode, with a few favourite books, in a cottage, somewhere within sight of the church steeple peeping out among the old elms, and within the sound of its solemn bells. For to me there is something strangely fascinat-

48

ing in an English village church. The grey time-worn
walls, with their mosses and lichens and weather-stains,
the very bareness and simplicity of the whitewashed
interior with its plain pews and unpretending pulpit, the
silence that reigns within when you enter on a week-day,
the sight of the green leaves fluttering outside in the
breeze, the sweet scent of the hawthorn or the hay blown
in upon you through the open windows or door, make
up an impression, or rather a series of impressions, well
fitted to ease the troubled or jaded mind, to wear away
its carking cares, to smooth out, if I may say so, its
creases and rumples, in a word, to restore its composure
and calm. And the charm of a village church is greatly
enhanced when, as here at Coverley, it adjoins an
ancient Hall, the two together carrying the mind back
into the past, to England of the olden time, which,
whether justly or not, in the bustle of modern life we
regard with a certain fond regret. The world, we are
fain to think, went very well then; though, to be candid,
I imagine that if the kindly wizard Time, who spreads
enchantment over distant views, were to transport us to
those vanished scenes, we might find the spell broken
and ourselves disenchanted.

However that may be, the longer I stay at the Hall,
the more I love its master. For there is about him a
sweet simplicity, a sort of childlike frankness and
innocence which wonderfully pleases me and puts me
many times in mind of Our Saviour's words, " Suffer
the little children to come unto me, and forbid them
not; for of such is the kingdom of heaven." I think I
never met one who seemed to me to need less preparation
for death and for that communion with the spirits of

the just made perfect, to which Scripture teaches us to look forward as a principal source of the happiness that awaits us in the life hereafter. Not that Sir Roger is either very wise or very witty; for in truth he is neither, unless, as I am sometimes prone to think, the greatest wisdom consists in the greatest purity of the heart, for judged by that standard I would be bold to match Sir Roger against Socrates or any sage in history.

As he has arrived at the time of life when men naturally turn their thoughts to the long past that is behind them rather than to the short and uncertain future before them, Sir Roger loves to recall the memories of his youth, and in this propensity I encourage him, for he has much to tell of stirring scenes that he witnessed in days when England was more agitated than now and had not yet attained to that settled state of internal tranquillity for which we are indebted to the prudence and vigilance of Her present Most Gracious Majesty. He remembers faintly as in a dream the dismal pageantry of the day when the remains of the usurper, who styled himself Protector, were borne, with more than regal solemnity, amid the silence of an innumerable throng, to rest with the dust of kings and princes. He recalls more distinctly and with far greater pleasure, the wild outburst of joy which greeted the return of His Majesty King Charles the Second; how the streets were strewed with flowers and hung with tapestry; how the windows and balconies were crowded with ladies; how bells rang, trumpets blared, and fountains ran wine; and how the horse and foot, with shouts and brandishing of swords, the Livery Companies with their chains of gold and banners, and lords and nobles clad in cloth of silver and velvet, were passing for hours the place where he stood in the Strand to watch them. As a young man he witnessed the Great Plague and the Great Fire of London, and he well remembers the sad day when the roar of the Dutch guns in the Thames was heard like the rumble of thunder all over the city, the people in a dreadful suspense crowding into the streets to listen, till the sullen sound of the firing drew farther and farther off, and finally died away in the distance.

Yesterday Sir Roger was in a particularly communicative vein. The day was hot, and in the afternoon we walked out through the fields by a footpath beside a high hedge and in the dappled shade of a long row of venerable elms; then crossing a meadow and passing through the churchyard of a little hamlet, where the grassy mounds and mossy headstones basked in the sunshine among ancient yews, we ascended the slope of a hill by a track that led through tall wheat, now turned a rich russet brown and spangled with scarlet poppies. Thus ascending we reached the brow of the hill and struck a high road which here runs for miles along the crest of the ridge, skirted on the one side by a wood and on the other hand affording wide views down the declivity and away over the flat country to some low blue hills which bound the prospect in the far distance. Just on the brow of the hill there stands a ruinous old windmill, its timbers rotting and its great sails drooping like the wings of a wounded bird. Here on a bench we sat down to rest and to enjoy the freshness of the air on the height before retracing our steps homeward. The landscape spread out before us was peaceful and pleasing. At our feet the high road ran steeply down the slope, and where it passed out of sight we could still trace its line by the trees that fringed it on either side, rising and sinking like a green wave with the undulations of the ground. Away to the north, faintly discernible as specks on the horizon, appeared the towers of a minster, but so far off that they would have escaped me if Sir Roger had not pointed them out. In the foreground, but still at a distance of several miles, we could see the woods of Coverley, and just over the edge of the hill the spire of the little village church which we had passed before ascending the slope. On the side of the distant blue hills, beyond the woods of Coverley, my friend bade me mark what looked like a white scar; he said it was the high road to Oxford.

Charmed, as it were, by the prospect we sat a long time, and Sir Roger chatted of other days, while I listened spellbound, till the sun, sinking in the west, stretched out the shadows on the slope of the hill and reminded us that it was time to return. So, rising reluctantly, we descended the hill and followed the high road back to Coverley. What the old knight told me, as we sat there that summer evening, will long remain imprinted on my memory, and may furnish matter for the future entertainment of my readers. But their patience, like my paper, is no doubt exhausted, and I will not tax it further to-day.

SIR JAMES GEORGE FRAZER—*The Gorgon's Head.*

A CHINESE TALE

MANKIND, says a Chinese manuscript, which my friend
M.[1] was obliging enough to read and explain to me, for
the first seventy thousand ages ate their meat raw, claw-
ing or biting it from the living animal, just as they do
in Abyssinia to this day. This period is not obscurely
hinted at by their great Confucius in the second chapter
of his Mundane Mutations, where he designates a kind
of golden age by the term Cho-fang, literally the Cook's
holiday. The manuscript goes on to say, that the art
of roasting, or rather broiling (which I take to be the
elder brother) was accidentally discovered in the manner
following. The swine-herd, Ho-ti, having gone out into
the woods one morning, as his manner was, to collect
mast for his hogs, left his cottage in the care of his eldest
son Bo-bo, a great lubberly boy, who being fond of playing with fire, as younkers of his age commonly are, let
some sparks escape into a bundle of straw, which
kindling quickly, spread the conflagration over every
part of their poor mansion, till it was reduced to ashes.
Together with the cottage (a sorry antediluvian make-

[1] Thomas Manning.

shift of a building, you may think it), what was of much more importance, a fine litter of new-farrowed pigs, no less than nine in number, perished. China pigs have been esteemed a luxury all over the East from the remotest periods that we read of. Bo-bo was in utmost consternation, as you may think, not so much for the sake of the tenement, which his father and he could easily build up again with a few dry branches, and the labour of an hour or two, at any time, as for the loss of the pigs. While he was thinking what he should say to his father, and wringing his hands over the smoking remnants of one of those untimely sufferers, an odour assailed his nostrils, unlike any scent which he had before experienced. What could it proceed from?—not from the burnt cottage—he had smelt that smell before —indeed this was by no means the first accident of the kind which had occurred through the negligence of this unlucky young fire-brand. Much less did it resemble that of any known herb, weed or flower. A premonitory moistening at the same time overflowed his nether lip. He knew not what to think. He next stooped down to feel the pig, if there were any signs of life in it. He burnt his fingers, and to cool them he applied them in his booby fashion to his mouth. Some of the crumbs of the scorched skin had come away with his fingers, and for the first time in his life (in the world's life indeed, for before him no man had known it) he tasted— *crackling*! Again he felt and fumbled at the pig. It did not burn him so much now, still he licked his fingers from a sort of habit. The truth at length broke into his slow understanding, that it was the pig that smelt so, and the pig that tasted so delicious; and, surrendering himself up to the new-born pleasure, he fell to tearing up whole handfuls of the scorched skin with the flesh next it, and was cramming it down his throat in his beastly fashion, when his sire entered amid the smoking rafters, armed with retributory cudgel, and finding how affairs stood, began to rain blows upon the young rogue's shoulders, as thick as hail-stones, which Bo-bo heeded not any more than if they had been flies. The tickling pleasure which he experienced in his lower regions, had rendered him quite callous to any inconveniences he might feel in those remote quarters. His father might lay on, but he could not beat him from his pig, till he had fairly made an end of it, when, becoming a little more sensible of his situation, something like the following dialogue ensued.

"You graceless whelp, what have you got there devouring? Is it not enough that you have burnt me down three houses with your dog's tricks, and be hanged to you, but you must be eating fire, and I know not what —what have you got there, I say?"

"O father, the pig, the pig, do come and taste how nice the burnt pig eats."

The ears of Ho-ti tingled with horror. He cursed his son, and he cursed himself that ever he should beget a son that should eat burnt pig.

Bo-bo, whose scent was wonderfully sharpened since morning, soon raked out another pig, and fairly rending it asunder, thrust the lesser half by main force into the fists of Ho-ti, still shouting out, "Eat, eat, eat the burnt pig, father, only taste—O Lord,"—with such-like barbarous ejaculations, cramming all the while as if he would choke.

Ho-ti trembled in every joint while he grasped the abominable thing, wavering whether he should not put his son to death for an unnatural young monster, when the crackling scorching his fingers, as it had done his son's, and applying the same remedy to them, he in his turn tasted some of its flavour, which, make what sour mouths he would for a pretence, proved not altogether displeasing to him. In conclusion (for the manuscript here is a little tedious), both father and son fairly sat down to the mess, and never left off till they had dispatched all that remained of the litter.

Bo-bo was strictly enjoined not to let the secret escape, for the neighbours would certainly have stoned them for a couple of abominable wretches, who could think of improving upon the good meat which God had sent them. Nevertheless, strange stories got about. It was observed that Ho-ti's cottage was burnt down now more frequently than ever. Nothing but fires from this time forward. Some would break out in broad day, others in the night-time. As often as the sow farrowed, so sure was the house of Ho-ti to be in a blaze; and Ho-ti himself, which was the more remarkable, instead of chastising his son, seemed to grow more indulgent to him than ever. At length they were watched, the terrible mystery discovered, and father and son summoned to take their trial at Pekin, then an inconsiderable assize town. Evidence was given, the obnoxious food itself produced in court, and verdict about to be pronounced, when the foreman of the jury begged that some of the burnt pig, of which the culprits stood accused, might be handed into the box. He handled it, and they all handled it, and burning their fingers, as

Bo-bo and his father had done before them, and nature prompting to each of them the same remedy, against the face of all the facts, and the clearest charge which judge had ever given—to the surprise of the whole court, townsfolk, strangers, reporters, and all present—without leaving the box, or any manner of consultation whatever, they brought in a simultaneous verdict of Not Guilty.

The judge, who was a shrewd fellow, winked at the manifest iniquity of the decision: and, when the court was dismissed, went privily, and bought up all the pigs that could be had for love or money. In a few days his Lordship's town house was observed to be on fire. The thing took wing, and now there was nothing to be seen but fires in every direction. Fuel and pigs grew enormously dear all over the district. The insurance offices one and all shut up shop. People built slighter and slighter every day, until it was feared that the very science of architecture would in no long time be lost to the world. Thus this custom of firing houses continued, till in process of time, says my manuscript, a sage arose, like our Locke, who made a discovery, that the flesh of swine, or indeed of any other animal, might be cooked (burnt, as they called it) without the necessity of consuming a whole house to dress it. Then first began the rude form of a grid-iron. Roasting by the string, or spit, came in a century or two later, I forget in whose dynasty. By such slow degrees, concludes the manuscript, do the most useful, and seemingly the most obvious arts, make their way among mankind.

Without placing too implicit faith in the account

above given, it must be agreed, that if a worthy pretext for so dangerous an experiment as setting houses on fire (especially in these days) could be assigned in favour of any culinary object, that pretext and excuse might be found in ROAST PIG.

CHARLES LAMB—*The Essays of Elia.* (*A Dissertation on Roast Pig* [abridged])

MY FRIEND THE PIG

Is there a man among us who on running through a
list of his friends is unable to say that there is one
among them who is a perfect pig? I think not; and if
any reader says that he has no such an one for the
simple reason that he would not and could not make a
friend of a perfect pig, I shall maintain that he is mis-
taken, that if he goes over the list a second time and a
little more carefully, he will find in it not only a pig,
but a sheep, a cow, a fox, a cat, a stoat, and even a
perfect toad.

But all this is a question I am not concerned with,
seeing that the pig I wish to write about is a real one—
a four-footed beast with parted hoofs. I have a friendly
feeling towards pigs generally, and consider them the
most intelligent of beasts, not excepting the elephant
and the anthropoid ape—the dog is not to be mentioned
in this connection. I also like his disposition and
attitude towards all other creatures, especially man. He
is not suspicious, or shrinkingly submissive, like horses,
cattle and sheep; nor an impudent devil-may-care like
the goat; nor hostile like the goose; nor condescending
like the cat; nor a flattering parasite like the dog. He

views us from a totally different, a sort of democratic, standpoint as fellow-citizens and brothers, and takes it for granted, or grunted, that we understand his language, and without servility or insolence he has a natural, pleasant, camerados-all or hail-fellow-well-met air with us.

It may come as a shock to some of my readers when I add that I like him, too, in the form of rashers on the breakfast-table; and this I say with a purpose on account of much wild and idle talk one hears on this question even from one's dearest friends—the insincere horror expressed and denunciation of the revolting custom of eating our fellow-mortals. The other day a lady of my acquaintance told me that she went to call on some people who lived a good distance from her house, and was obliged to stay to luncheon. This consisted mainly of roast pork, and as if that was not enough, her host, when helping her, actually asked if she was fond of a dreadful thing called the crackling!

It is a common pose; but it is also something more, since we find it mostly in persons who are frequently in bad health and are restricted to a low diet; naturally at such times vegetarianism appeals to them. As their health improves they think less of their fellow-mortals. A little chicken broth is found uplifting; then follows the inevitable sole, then calves' brains, then a sweet-bread, then a partridge, and so on, progressively, until they are once more able to enjoy their salmon or turbot, veal and lamb cutlets, fat capons, turkeys and geese, sirloins of beef, and, finally, roast pig. That's the limit; we have outgrown cannibalism, and are not keen about haggis, though it is still eaten by the wild tribes inhabit-

ing the northern portion of our island. All this should
serve to teach vegetarians not to be in a hurry.
Thoreau's " handful of rice " is not sufficient for us, and
not good enough yet. It will take long years and
centuries of years before the wolf with blood on his iron
jaws can be changed into the white innocent lamb that
nourishes itself on grass.

Let us now return to my friend the pig. He inhabited
a stye at the far end of the back garden of a cottage or
small farmhouse in a lonely little village in the Wiltshire
downs where I was staying. Close to the stye was a gate
opening into a long green field, shut in by high hedges,
where two or three horses and four or five cows were
usually grazing. These beasts, not knowing my senti-
ments, looked askance at me and moved away when I
first began to visit them, but when they made the discovery that I generally had apples and lumps of sugar in
my coat-pockets they all at once became excessively
friendly and followed me about, and would put their
heads in my way to be scratched, and licked my hands
with their rough tongues to show that they liked me.
Every time I visited the cows and horses I had to pause
beside the pig-pen to open the gate into the field; and
invariably the pig would get up and coming towards me
salute me with a friendly grunt. And I would pretend
not to hear or see, for it made me sick to look at his
pen in which he stood belly-deep in the fetid mire, and
it made me ashamed to think that so intelligent and
good-tempered an animal, so profitable to man, should
be kept in such abominable conditions. Oh, poor beast,
excuse me, but I'm in a hurry and have no time to return
your greeting or even to look at you!

In this village, as in most of the villages in all this agricultural and pastoral county of Wiltshire, there is a pig-club, and many of the cottagers keep a pig; they think and talk a great deal about their pigs, and have a grand pig-day gathering and dinner, with singing and even dancing to follow, once a year. And no wonder that this is so, considering what they get out of the pig; yet in any village you will find it kept in this same unspeakable condition. It is not from indolence nor because they take pleasure in seeing their pig unhappy before killing him or sending him away to be killed, but because they cherish the belief that the filthier the state in which they keep their pig the better the pork will be! I have met even large prosperous farmers, many of them, who cling to this delusion. One can imagine a conversation between one of these Wiltshire pig-keepers and a Danish farmer. "Yes," the visitor would say, "we too had the same notion at one time, and thought it right to keep our pigs as you do; but that was a long time back, when English and Danes were practically one people, seeing that Canute was king of both countries. We have since then adopted a different system; we now believe, and the results prove that we are in the right way, that it is best to consider the animal's nature and habits and wants, and to make the artificial conditions imposed on him as little oppressive as may be. It is true that in a state of nature the hog loves to go into pools and wallow in the mire, just as stags, buffaloes, and many other beasts do, especially in the dog-days when the flies are most troublesome. But the swine, like the stag, is a forest animal, and does not love filth for its own sake nor to be left in a miry pen, and though

not as fastidious as a cat about his coat, he is naturally
as clean as any other forest creature."

Here I may add that in scores of cases when I have
asked a cottager why he didn't keep a pig, his answer
has been that he would gladly do so, but for the sanitary
inspectors, who would soon order him to get rid of it,
or remove it to a distance on account of the offensive
smell. It is probable that if it could be got out of the
cottager's mind that there must needs be an offensive
smell, the number of pigs fattened in the villages would
be trebled.

I hope now after all these digressions I shall be able to
go on with the history of my friend the pig. One morning as I passed the pen he grunted—spoke, I may say—
in such a pleasant friendly way that I had to stop and
return his greeting; then, taking an apple from my
pocket, I placed it in his trough. He turned it over
with his snout, then looked up and said something like
"Thank-you" in a series of gentle grunts. Then he
bit off and ate a small piece, then another small bite, and
eventually taking what was left in his mouth he finished
eating it. After that he always expected me to stay a
minute and speak to him when I went to the field; I
knew it from his way of greeting me, and on such occasions I gave him an apple. But he never ate it greedily:
he appeared more inclined to talk than to eat, until by
degrees I came to understand what he was saying.
What he said was that he appreciated my kind inten-
tions in giving him apples. But, he went on, to tell the
real truth, it is not a fruit I am particularly fond of. I
am familiar with its taste as they sometimes give me
apples, usually the small unripe or bad ones that fall

from the trees. However, I don't actually dislike them. I get skim milk and am rather fond of it; then a bucket of mash, which is good enough for hunger; but what I enjoy most is a cabbage, only I don't get one very often now. I sometimes think that if they would let me out of this muddy pen to ramble like the sheep and other beasts in the field or on the downs I should be able to pick up a number of morsels which would taste better than anything they give me. Apart from the subject of food, I hope you won't mind my telling you that I'm rather fond of being scratched on the back.

So I scratched him vigorously with my stick, and made him wriggle his body and wink and blink and smile delightedly all over his face. Then I said to myself: " Now what the juice can I do more to please him? " For though under sentence of death, he had done no wrong, but was a good, honest-hearted fellow-mortal, so that I felt bound to do something to make the miry remnant of his existence a little less miserable.

I think it was the word *juice* I had just used—for that was how I pronounced it to make it less like a swear-word—that gave me an inspiration. In the garden, a few yards back from the pen, there was a large clump of old elder-trees, now overloaded with ripening fruit— the biggest clusters I had ever seen. Going to the trees I selected and cut the finest bunch I could find, as big and round as my cap, and weighing over a pound. This I deposited in his trough and invited him to try it. He sniffed at it a little doubtfully, and looked at me and made a remark or two, then nibbled at the edge of the cluster, taking a few berries into his mouth, and holding

64

them some time before he ventured to crush them. At
length he did venture, then looked at me again and
made more remarks, " Queer fruit this! Never tasted
anything quite like it before, but I really can't say yet
whether I like it or not."

Then he took another bite, then more bites, looking
up at me, and saying something between the bites, till,
little by little, he had consumed the whole bunch; then
turning round, he went back to his bed with a little grunt
to say that I was now at liberty to go on to the cows and
horses.

However, on the following morning he hailed my
approach in such a lively manner, with such a note of
expectancy in his voice, that I concluded he had been
thinking a great deal about elder-berries, and was
anxious to have another go at them. Accordingly I cut
him another bunch, which he quickly consumed, making little exclamations the while—" Thank you, thank
you, very good—very good indeed! " It was a new
sensation in his life, and made him very happy, and was
almost as good as a day of liberty in the fields and
meadows and on the open green downs.

From that time I visited him two or three times a day
to give him huge clusters of elder-berries. There were
plenty for the starlings as well; the clusters on those trees
would have filled a cart.

Then one morning I heard an indignant scream from
the garden, and peeping out saw my friend the pig,
bound hand and foot, being lifted by a dealer into his
cart with the assistance of the farmer.

" Good-bye, old boy! " said I as the cart drove off;
and I thought that by and by, in a month or two, if

several persons discovered a peculiar and fascinating flavour in their morning rasher, it would be due to the elder-berries I had supplied to my friend the pig, which had gladdened his heart for a week or two before receiving his quietus.

W. H. HUDSON—*The Book of a Naturalist.*

ANGLING AND AN ANGLER

It is said that many an unlucky urchin is induced to run away from his family, and betake himself to a seafaring life, from reading the history of Robinson Crusoe; and I suspect that, in like manner, many of those worthy gentlemen who are given to haunt the sides of pastoral streams with angle rods in hand, may trace the origin of their passion to the seductive pages of honest Izaak Walton. I recollect studying his *Compleat Angler* several years since, in company with a knot of friends in America, and, moreover, that we were all completely bitten with the angling mania. It was early in the year; but as soon as the weather was auspicious, and that the spring began to melt into the verge of summer, we took rod in hand and sallied into the country, as stark mad as was ever Don Quixote from reading books of chivalry.

One of our party had equalled the Don in the fulness of his equipments, being attired *cap-à-pie* for the enterprise. He wore a broad-skirted fustian coat, perplexed with half a hundred pockets; a pair of stout shoes, and leather gaiters; a basket slung on one side for fish; a patent rod, a landing-net, and a score of other inconveniences, only to be found in the true angler's armoury. Thus harnessed for the field, he was as great a matter of stare and wonderment among the country folk, who had never seen a regular angler, as was the steel-clad hero of La Mancha among the goatherds of the Sierra Morena.

Our first essay was along a mountain brook, among the highlands of the Hudson; a most unfortunate place for the execution of those piscatory tactics which had been invented along the velvet margins of quiet English rivulets. It was one of those wild streams that lavish, among our romantic solitudes, unheeded beauties, enough to fill the sketch-book of a hunter of the picturesque. Sometimes it would leap down rocky shelves, making small cascades, over which the trees threw their broad balancing sprays, and long nameless weeds hung in fringes from the impending banks, dripping with diamond drops. Sometimes it would brawl and fret along a ravine in the matted shade of a forest, filling it with murmurs; and, after this termagant career, would steal forth into open day with the most placid demure face imaginable; as I have seen some pestilent shrew of a housewife, after filling her home with uproar and ill-humour, come dimpling out of doors, swimming and courtesying, and smiling upon all the world.

How smoothly would this vagrant brook glide, at such times, through some bosom of green meadow-land among the mountains; where the quiet was only interrupted by the occasional tinkling of a bell from the lazy cattle among the clover, or the sound of a woodcutter's axe from the neighbouring forest.

For my part, I was always a bungler at all kinds of sport that required either patience or adroitness, and had not angled above half an hour before I had completely " satisfied the sentiment," and convinced myself of the truth of Izaak Walton's opinion, that angling is something like poetry—a man must be born to it. I hooked myself instead of the fish; tangled my line in every tree; lost my bait; broke my rod; until I gave up the attempt in despair, and passed the day under the trees, reading old Izaak; satisfied that it was his fascinating vein of honest simplicity and rural feeling that had bewitched me, and not the passion for angling. My companions, however, were more persevering in their delusion. I have them at this moment before my eyes, stealing along the border of the brook, where it lay open to the day, or was merely fringed by shrubs and bushes. I see the bittern rising with hollow scream as they break in upon his rarely invaded haunt; the kingfisher watching them suspiciously from his dry tree that overhangs the deep black mill-pond in the gorge of the hills; the tortoise letting himself slip sideways from off the stone or log on which he is sunning himself; and the panic-struck frog plumping in headlong as they approach, and spreading an alarm throughout the watery world around.

I recollect, also, that, after toiling and watching and creeping about for the greater part of a day, with scarcely any success, in spite of all our admirable apparatus, a lubberly country urchin came down from the hills with a rod made from a branch of a tree, a few yards of twine, and, as heaven shall help me! I believe a crooked pin for a hook, baited with a vile earthworm—and in half an hour caught more fish than we had nibbles throughout the day!

But, above all, I recollect the " good, honest, wholesome, hungry " repast, which we made under a beech-tree, just by a spring of pure sweet water that stole out of the side of a hill; and how, when it was over, one of the party read old Izaak Walton's scene with the milkmaid, while I lay on the grass and built castles in a bright pile of clouds, until I fell asleep. All this may appear like mere egotism; yet I cannot refrain from uttering these recollections, which are passing like a strain of music over my mind, and have been called up by an agreeable scene which I witnessed not long since.

In a morning stroll along the banks of the Alun, a beautiful little stream which flows down from the Welsh hills, and throws itself into the Dee, my attention was attracted to a group seated on the margin. On approaching, I found it to consist of a veteran angler and two rustic disciples. The former was an old fellow with a wooden leg, with clothes very much but very carefully patched, betokening poverty, honestly come by, and decently maintained. His face bore the marks of former storms, but present fair weather; its furrows had been worn into an habitual smile; his iron-grey locks hung about his ears, and he had altogether the good-humoured air of a constitutional philosopher who was disposed to take the world as it went. One of his companions was a ragged wight, with the skulking look of an arrant poacher, and I warrant could find his way to any gentleman's fish-pond in the neighbourhood in the darkest night. The other was a tall, awkward, country lad, with a lounging gait, and apparently somewhat of a rustic beau. The old man was busy in examining the maw of a trout which he had just killed, to discover by its contents what insects were seasonable for bait; and was lecturing on the subject to his companions, who appeared to listen with infinite deference. I have a kind feeling towards all " brothers of the angle," ever since I read Izaak Walton. They are men, he affirms, of a " mild, sweet and peaceable spirit "; and my esteem for them has been increased since I met with an old *Tretyse of Fishing with the Angle*, in which are set forth many of the maxims of their inoffensive fraternity. " Take good hede," sayeth this honest little tretyse, " that in going about your disportes ye open no man's gates, but that ye shet them again. Also ye shall not use this forsayd crafti disport for no covetousness to the encreasing and sparing of your money only, but principally for your solace, and to cause the helth of your body and specyally of your soule."[1]

I thought that I could perceive in the veteran angler before me an exemplification of what I had read; and there was a cheerful contentedness in his looks that quite drew me towards him. I could not but remark the gallant manner in which he stumped from one part of the brook to another; waving his rod in the air, to keep the line from dragging on the ground, or catching among the bushes; and the adroitness with which he would throw his fly to any particular place; sometimes skimming it lightly along a little rapid; sometimes casting it into one of those dark holes made by a twisted root or overhanging bank, in which the large trout are apt to lurk. In the meanwhile he was giving instructions to

[1] From this same treatise, it would appear that angling is a more industrious and devout employment than it is generally considered. —" For when ye purpose to go on your disportes in fishynge ye will not desyre greatlye many persons with you, which might let you of your game. And that ye may serve God devoutly in sayinge effectually your customable prayers. And thus doying, ye shall eschew and also avoyde many vices, as ydelnes, which is principall cause to induce man to many other vices, as it is right well known."

his two disciples; showing them the manner in which they should handle their rods, fix their flies, and play them along the surface of the stream. The scene brought to my mind the instructions of the sage Piscator to his scholar. The country around was of that pastoral kind which Walton is fond of describing. It was a part of the great plain of Cheshire, close by the beautiful vale of Gessford, and just where the inferior Welsh hills begin to swell up from among fresh-smelling meadows. The day, too, like that recorded in his work, was mild and sunshiny, with now and then a soft-dropping shower, that sowed the whole earth with diamonds.

I soon fell into conversation with the old angler, and was so much entertained, that, under pretext of receiving instructions in his art, I kept company with him almost the whole day; wandering along the banks of the stream, and listening to his talk. He was very communicative, having all the easy garrulity of cheerful old age; and I fancy was a little flattered by having an opportunity of displaying his piscatory lore; for who does not like now and then to play the sage?

He had been much of a rambler in his day, and had passed some years of his youth in America, particularly in Savannah, where he had entered into trade and had been ruined by the indiscretion of a partner. He had afterwards experienced many ups and downs in life, until he got into the navy, where his leg was carried away by a cannon-ball, at the battle of Camperdown. This was the only stroke of real good fortune he had ever experienced, for it got him a pension, which, together with some small paternal property, brought him in a revenue of nearly forty pounds. On this he retired to his native village, where he lived quietly and independently; and devoted the remainder of his life to the "noble art of angling."

I found that he had read Izaak Walton attentively, and he seemed to have imbibed all his simple frankness and prevalent good humour. Though he had been sorely buffeted about the world, he was satisfied that the world, in itself, was good and beautiful. Though he had been so roughly used in different countries, as a poor sheep that is fleeced by every hedge and thicket, yet he spoke of every nation with candour and kindness, appearing to look only on the good side of things; and, above all, he was almost the only man I had ever met with who had been an unfortunate adventurer in America, and had honesty and magnanimity enough to take the fault to his own door, and not to curse the country. The lad that was receiving his instructions, I learnt, was the son and heir apparent of a fat old widow who kept the village inn, and, of course, a youth of some expectation, and much courted by the idle gentleman-like personages of the place. In taking him under his care, therefore, the old man had probably an eye to a privileged corner in the taproom, and an occasional cup of cheerful ale free of expense.

There is certainly something in angling, if we could forget, which anglers are apt to do, the cruelties and tortures inflicted on worms and insects, that tends to produce a gentleness of spirit, and a pure serenity of mind. As the English are methodical, even in their recreations, and are the most scientific of sportsmen, it has been reduced among them to perfect rule and system. Indeed, it is an amusement peculiarly adapted to the mild and

73

c*

highly cultivated scenery of England, where every roughness has been softened away from the landscape. It is delightful to saunter along those limpid streams which wander, like veins of silver, through the bosom of this beautiful country; leading one through a diversity of small home scenery; sometimes winding through ornamented grounds; sometimes brimming along through rich pasturage, where the fresh green is mingled with sweet-smelling flowers; sometimes venturing in sight of villages and hamlets, and then running capriciously away into shady retirements. The sweetness and serenity of nature, and the quiet watchfulness of the sport, gradually bring on pleasant fits of musing, which are now and then agreeably interrupted by the song of a bird, the distant whistle of the peasant, or perhaps, the vagary of some fish, leaping out of the still water, and skimming transiently about its glassy surface. " When I would beget content," says Izaak Walton, " and increase confidence in the power and wisdom and providence of Almighty God, I will walk the meadows by some gliding stream, and there contemplate the lilies that take no care, and those very many other little living creatures that are not only created, but fed (man knows not how) by the goodness of the God of nature, and therefore trust in him."

I cannot forbear to give another quotation from one of those ancient champions of angling, which breathes the same innocent and happy spirit:

Let me live harmlessly, and near the brink
Of Trent or Avon have a dwelling-place,
Where I may see my quill, or cork, down sink
With eager bite of pike, or bleak, or dace;

And on the world and my Creator think:
  Whilst some men strive ill-gotten goods t'embrace;
And others spend their time in base excess
  Of wine, or worse, in war, or wantonness.
Let them that will, these pastimes still pursue,
  And on such pleasing fancies feed their fill;
So I the fields and meadows green may view,
  And daily by fresh rivers walk at will,
Among the daisies and the violets blue,
  Red hyacinth and yellow daffodil.[1]

On parting with the old angler, I inquired after his place of abode, and happening to be in the neighbourhood of the village a few evenings afterwards, I had the curiosity to seek him out. I found him living in a small cottage, containing only one room, but a perfect curiosity in its method and arrangement. It was on the skirts of the village, on a green bank, a little back from the road, with a small garden in front, stocked with kitchen herbs, and adorned with a few flowers. The whole front of the cottage was overrun with a honeysuckle. On the top was a ship for a weathercock. The interior was fitted up in a truly nautical style, his ideas of comfort and convenience having been acquired on the berth-deck of a man-of-war. A hammock was slung from the ceiling, which, in the daytime, was lashed up so as to take but little room. From the centre of the chamber hung a model of a ship, of his own workmanship. Two or three chairs, a table and a large sea-chest formed the principal movables. About the wall were stuck up naval ballads, such as " Admiral Hosier's Ghost," " All in the Downs," and " Tom Bowling," intermingled with pic-

[1] J. Davors.

tures of sea-fights, among which the battle of Camperdown held a distinguished place. The mantelpiece was decorated with sea-shells, over which hung a quadrant, flanked by two wood-cuts of most bitter-looking naval commanders. His implements for angling were carefully disposed on nails and hooks about the room. On a shelf was arranged his library, containing a work on angling, much worn, a Bible covered with canvas, an old volume or two of voyages, a nautical almanack, and a book of songs.

His family consisted of a large black cat with one eye, and a parrot which he had caught and tamed, and educated himself, in the course of one of his voyages; and which uttered a variety of sea phrases with the hoarse brattling tone of a veteran boatswain. The establishment reminded me of that of the renowned Robinson Crusoe; it was kept in neat order, everything being " stowed away " with the regularity of a ship of war; and he informed me that he " scoured the deck every morning, and swept it between meals."

I found him seated on a bench before the door, smoking his pipe in the soft evening sunshine. His cat was purring soberly on the threshold, and his parrot describing some strange evolutions in an iron ring that swung in the centre of his cage. He had been angling all day, and gave me a history of his sport with as much minuteness as a general would talk over a campaign; being particularly animated in relating the manner in which he had taken a large trout, which had completely tasked all his skill and wariness, and which he had sent as a trophy to mine hostess of the inn.

How comforting it is to see a cheerful and contented old age; and to behold a poor fellow, like this, after being tempest-tost through life, safely moored in a snug and quiet harbour in the evening of his days! His happiness, however, sprung from within himself, and was independent of external circumstances; for he had that inexhaustible good nature, which is the most precious gift of heaven; spreading itself like oil over the troubled sea of thought, and keeping the mind smooth and equable in the roughest weather.

On inquiring further about him, I learnt that he was a universal favourite in the village, and the oracle of the taproom; where he delighted the rustics with his songs, and, like Sinbad, astonished them with his stories of strange lands, and shipwrecks, and sea-fights. He was much noticed, too, by gentlemen sportsmen of the neighbourhood; had taught several of them the art of angling; and was a privileged visitor to their kitchens. The whole tenor of his life was quiet and inoffensive, being principally passed about the neighbouring streams, when the weather and season were favourable; and at other times he employed himself at home, preparing his fishing tackle for the next campaign, or manufacturing rods, nets, and flies, for his patrons and pupils among the gentry.

He was a regular attendant at church on Sundays, though he generally fell asleep during the sermon. He had made it his particular request that when he died he should be buried in a green spot, which he could see from his seat in church, and which he had marked out ever since he was a boy, and had thought of when far from home on the raging sea, in danger of being food

77

for the fishes—it was the spot where his father and mother had been buried.

I have done, for I fear that my reader is growing weary; but I could not refrain from drawing the picture of this worthy " brother of the angle "; who has made me more than ever in love with the theory, though I fear I shall never be adroit in the practice, of his art; and I will conclude this rambling sketch in the words of honest Izaak Walton, by craving the blessing of St. Peter's master upon my reader, " and upon all that are true lovers of virtue; and dare trust in His providence: and be quiet; and go a-angling."

WASHINGTON IRVING—*The Sketch Book of Geoffrey Crayon, Gent.*

A COUNTRY CRICKET MATCH

For the last three weeks our village has been in a state of great excitement, occasioned by a challenge from our north-western neighbours, the men of B., to contend with us at cricket. Now we have not been much in the habit of playing matches. Three or four years ago indeed, we encountered the men of S., our neighbours south-by-east, with a sort of doubtful success, beating them on our own ground, whilst they in the second match returned the compliment on theirs. This discouraged us. Then an unnatural coalition between a high-church curate and an evangelical gentleman-farmer drove our lads from the Sunday evening practice, which, as it did not begin before both services were concluded, and as it tended to keep the young men from the ale-house, our magistrates had winked at, if not encouraged. The sport therefore had languished until the present season, when under another change of circumstances the spirit began to revive. Half a dozen fine active lads, of influence amongst their comrades, grew into men and yearned for cricket; an enterprising publican gave a set of ribands: his rival, mine host of the Rose, an out-doer by profession, gave two; and the clergyman and his lay ally, both well-disposed and good-

natured men, gratified by the submission to their
authority, and finding, perhaps, that no great good
resulted from the substitution of public houses for out-
of-door diversions, relaxed. In short the practice recom-
menced, and the hill was again alive with men and boys,
and innocent merriment; but farther than the riband
matches amongst ourselves nobody dreamed of going,
till this challenge—we were modest, and doubted our
own strength. The B. people, on the other hand, must
have been braggers born, a whole parish of gasconaders.
Never was such boasting! such crowing! such ostenta-
tious display of practice! such mutual compliments from
man to man—bowler to batter, batter to bowler! It
was a wonder they did not challenge all England. It
must be confessed that we were a little astounded; yet
we firmly resolved not to decline the combat; and one
of the most spirited of the new growth, William Grey
by name, took up the glove in a style of manly courtesy,
that would have done honour to a knight in the days of
chivalry.—" We were not professed players," he said;
" being little better than schoolboys, and scarcely older;
but, since they had done us the honour to challenge us,
we would try our strength. It would be no discredit to
be beaten by such a field."

Having accepted the wager of battle, our champion
began forthwith to collect his forces. William Grey
is himself one of the finest youths that one shall see
—tall, active, slender and yet strong, with a piercing
eye full of sagacity, and a smile full of good humour,
—a farmer's son by station, and used to hard work as
farmers' sons are now, liked by everybody, and admitted
to be an excellent cricketer. He immediately set forth

to muster his men, remembering with great complacency that Samuel Long, a bowler *comme il y en a peu*, the very man who had knocked down nine wickets, had beaten us, bowled us out at the fatal return match some years ago at S., had luckily in a remove of a quarter of a mile last Lady-day, crossed the boundaries of his old parish, and actually belonged to us. Here was a stroke of good fortune! Our captain applied to him instantly; and he agreed at a word. Indeed Samuel Long is a very civilized person. He is a middle-aged man, who looks rather old amongst our young lads, and whose thickness and breadth give no token of remarkable activity; but he is very active, and so steady a player! so safe! We had half gained the match when we had secured him. He is a man of substance, too, in every way; owns one cow, two donkeys, six pigs, and geese and ducks beyond count;—dresses like a farmer, and owes no man a shilling;—and all this from pure industry, sheer day-labour. Note that your good cricketer is commonly the most industrious man in the parish; the habits that make him such are precisely those which make a good workman —steadiness, sobriety and activity—Samuel Long might pass for the *beau ideal* of the two characters. Happy were we to possess him! Then we had another piece of good luck. James Brown, a journeyman blacksmith and a native, who, being of a rambling disposition, had roamed from place to place for half a dozen years, had just returned to settle with his brother at another corner of our village, bringing with him a prodigious reputation in cricket and in gallantry—the gay Lothario of the neighbourhood. He is said to have made more conquests in love and in cricket than any blacksmith in the county. To him also went the indefatigable William Grey, and he also consented to play. No end to our good fortune! Another celebrated batter, called Joseph Hearne, had likewise recently married into the parish. He worked, it is true, at the A. mills, but slept at the house of his wife's father in our territories. He also was sought and found by our leader. But he was grand and shy; made an immense favour of the thing; courted courting and then hung back;—" Did not know that he could be spared; had partly resolved not to play again— at least not this season; thought it rash to accept the challenge; thought they might do without him——" —" Truly I think so too," said our spirited champion; " we will not trouble you, Mr. Hearne."

Having thus secured two powerful auxiliaries, and rejected a third, we began to reckon and select the regular native forces. Thus ran our list:—William Grey, 1.—Samuel Long, 2.—James Brown, 3.—George and John Simmons, one capital, the other so so,—an uncertain hitter, but a good fieldsman, 5.—Joel Brent, excellent, 6.—Ben Appleton—Here was a little pause— Ben's abilities at cricket were not completely ascertained; but then he was so good a fellow, so full of fun and waggery! no doing without Ben. So he figured in the list, 7.—George Harris—a short halt there too! Slowish —slow but sure. I think the proverb brought him in, 8.—Tom Coper—oh, beyond the world Tom Coper! the red-headed, gardening lad, whose left-handed strokes send *her* (a cricket ball, like that other moving thing a ship, is always of the feminine gender,) send her spin ning a mile, 9.—Harry Willis, another blacksmith, 10.

We had now ten of our eleven, but the choice of the

last occasioned some demur. Three young Martins, rich farmers of the neighbourhood, successively presented themselves, and were all rejected by our independent and impartial general for want of merit—*cricketal* merit. "Not good enough," was his pithy answer. Then our worthy neighbour, the half-pay lieutenant, offered his services—he, too, though with some hesitation and modesty, was refused—"Not quite young enough," was his sentence. John Strong, the exceeding long son of our dwarfish mason, was the next candidate —a nice youth—everybody likes John Strong—and a willing, but so tall and so limp, bent in the middle— a thread-paper, six feet high! We were all afraid that, in spite of his name, his strength would never hold out. "Wait till next year, John," quoth William Grey, with all the dignified seniority of twenty speaking to eighteen. "Coper's a year younger," said John. "Coper's a foot shorter," replied William: so John retired; and the eleventh man remained unchosen, almost to the eleventh hour. The eve of the match arrived, and the post was still vacant, when a little boy of fifteen, David Willis, brother to Harry, admitted by accident to the last practice, saw eight of them out, and was voted in by acclamation.

That Sunday evening's practice (for Monday was the important day) was a period of great anxiety, and, to say the truth, of great pleasure. There is something strangely delightful in the innocent spirit of the party. To be one of a numerous body, to be authorized to say *we*, to have a rightful interest in triumph or defeat, is gratifying at once to social feeling and to personal pride. There was not a ten-year-old urchin, or a septuagenary woman in the parish, who did not feel an additional importance, a reflected consequence, in speaking of " our side." An election interests in the same way; but that feeling is less pure. Money is there, and hatred, and politics, and lies. Oh, to be a voter, or a voter's wife, comes nothing near the genuine and hearty sympathy of belonging to a parish, breathing the same air, looking on the same trees, listening to the same nightingales! Talk of a patriotic elector!—Give me a parochial patriot, a man who loves his parish! Even we, the female partisans, may partake the common ardour. I am sure I did. I never, though tolerably eager and enthusiastic at all times, remember being in a more delicious state of excitement than on the eve of that battle. Our hopes waxed stronger and stronger. Those of our players who were present were excellent. William Grey got forty notches off his own bat; and that brilliant hitter, Tom Coper, gained eight from two successive balls. As the evening advanced, too, we had encouragement of another sort. A spy, who had been despatched to reconnoitre the enemy's quarters, returned from their practising ground with a most consolatory report. " Really," said Charles Grover, our intelligence—a fine old steady judge, one who had played well in his day—" they are no better than so many old women. Any five of ours would beat their eleven." This sent us to bed in high spirits.

Morning dawned less favourably. The sky promised a series of deluging showers, and kept its word as English skies are wont to do on such occasions; and a lamentable message arrived at the headquarters from our trusty comrade Joel Brent. His master, a great farmer, had begun the hay harvest that very morning, and Joel, being as eminent in one field as in another could not be spared. Imagine Joel's plight! the most ardent of all our eleven! a knight held back from the tourney! a soldier from the battle! The poor swain was inconsolable. At last, one who is always ready to do a good-natured action, great or little, set forth to back his petition; and, by dint of appealing to the public spirit of our worthy neighbour and the state of the barometer, talking alternately of the parish honour and thunder showers, of lost and sopped hay, he carried his point, and returned triumphantly with the delighted Joel.

In the meantime we became sensible of another defalcation. On calling over our roll, Brown was missing; and the spy of the preceding night, Charles Grover, —the universal scout and messenger of the village, a man who will run half a dozen miles for a pint of beer, who does errands for the very love of the trade, who, if he had been a lord, would have been an ambassador— was instantly despatched to summon the truant. His report spread general consternation. Brown had set off at four o'clock in the morning to play in a cricket match at M., a little town twelve miles off, which had been his last residence. Here was desertion! Here was treachery! Here was treachery against that goodly state, our parish! To send James Brown to Coventry was the immediate resolution; but even that seemed too light a punishment for such delinquency. Then how we cried him down! At ten on Sunday night (for the rascal had actually practised with us, and never said a word of his intended disloyalty) he was our faithful mate, and the best player (take him for all in all) of the eleven. At ten in the morning he had run away, and we were well

rid of him; he was no batter compared with William
Grey or Tom Coper; not fit to wipe the shoes of Samuel
Long, as a bowler; nothing of a scout to John Simmons;
the boy David Willis was worth fifty of him—

> " I trust we have within our realm
> Five hundred good as he,"

was the universal sentiment. So we took tall John
Strong, who, with an incurable hankering after the
honour of being admitted, had kept constantly with the
players, to take the chance of some such accident—we
took John for our *pis-aller*. I never saw anyone prouder
than the good-humoured lad was of this not very flattering piece of preferment.

John Strong was elected, and Brown sent to Coventry;
and, when I first heard of his delinquency, I thought
the punishment only too mild for the crime. But I have
since learned the secret history of the offence (if we could
know the secret histories of all offences, how much better
the world would seem than it does now!) and really my
wrath is much abated. It was a piece of gallantry, of
devotion to the sex, or rather a chivalrous obedience to
one chosen fair. I must tell my readers the story.
Mary Allen, the prettiest girl of M., had it seems
revenged upon our blacksmith the numberless incon-
sistencies of which he stood accused. He was in love
over head and ears, but the nymph was cruel. She said
no, and no, and no, and poor Brown, three times
rejected, at last resolved to leave the place, partly in
despair, and partly in that hope which often mingles
strangely with a lover's despair, the hope that when he
was gone he should be missed. He came home to his

brother's accordingly; but for five weeks he heard nothing from or of the inexorable Mary, and was glad to beguile his own " vexing thoughts," by endeavouring to create in his mind an artificial and factitious interest in our cricket match—all unimportant as such a trifle must have seemed to a man in love. Poor James, however, is a social and warm-hearted person, not likely to resist a contagious sympathy. As the time for the play advanced, the interest which he had at first affected became genuine and sincere; and he was really, when he left the ground on Sunday night, almost as enthusiastically absorbed in the event of the next day as Joel Brent himself. He little foresaw the new and delightful interest which awaited him at home, where, on the moment of his arrival, his sister-in-law and confidante presented him with a billet from the lady of his heart. It had, with the usual delay of letters sent by private hands in that rank of life, loitered on the road, in a degree inconceivable to those who are accustomed to the punctual speed of the post, and had taken ten days for its twelve miles' journey. Have my readers any wish to see this *billet-doux*? I can show them (but in strict confidence) a literal copy. It was addressed,

> " For mistur jem browne
> " blaxmith by
> " S."

The inside ran thus:—" Mistur browne this is to Inform yew that oure parish plays bramley men next monday is a week, i think we shall lose without yew, from your humbell servant to command
> " MARY ALLEN."

Was there ever a prettier relenting? a summons more flattering, more delicate, more irresistible? The precious epistle was undated; but having ascertained who brought it, and found by cross-examining the messenger, that the Monday in question was the very next day, we were not surprised to find that *Mistur browne* forgot his engagement to us, forgot all but Mary and Mary's letter, and set off at four o'clock the next morning to walk twelve miles, and play for her parish, and in her sight. Really we must not send James Brown to Coventry—must we? Though if, as his sister-in-law tells our damsel Harriet he hopes to do, he should bring the fair Mary home as his bride, he will not greatly care how little we say to him. But he must not be sent to Coventry—True-love forbid!

At last we were all assembled, and marched down to H. common, the appointed ground, which, though in our dominions according to the map, was the constant practising place of our opponents, and *terra incognita* to us. We found our adversaries on the ground as we expected, for our various delays had hindered us from taking the field so early as we wished; and, as soon as we had settled all preliminaries, the match began.

But alas! I have been so long settling my preliminaries, that I have left myself no room for the detail of our victory, and must squeeze the account of our grand achievements into as little compass as Cowley, when he crammed the names of eleven of his mistresses into the narrow space of four eight-syllable lines. *They* began the warfare—these boastful men of B. And what think you, gentle reader, was the amount of their innings? These challengers—the famous eleven—how many did

they get? Think! imagine! guess!—You cannot?—
Well!—they got twenty-two, or, rather, they got twenty;
for two of theirs were short notches, and would never
have been allowed, only that, seeing what they were
made of, we and our umpires were not particular.—
They should have had twenty more, if they had chosen
to claim them. Oh, how well we fielded! and how well
we bowled! our good play had quite as much to do with
their miserable failure as their bad. Samuel Long is a
slow bowler, George Simmons a fast one, and the change
from Long's lobbing to Simmons's fast balls posed them
completely. Poor simpletons! they were always wrong,
expecting the slow for the quick, and the quick for the
slow. Well, we went in. And what were our innings?
Guess again!—guess! A hundred and sixty-nine! in
spite of soaking showers, and wretched ground, where
the ball would not run a yard, we headed them by a
hundred and forty-seven; and then they gave in, as well
they might. William Grey pressed them much to try
another innings. "There was so much chance," as he
courteously observed, "in cricket, that advantageous as
our position seemed, we might, very possibly, be over-
taken. The B. men had better try." But they were
beaten sulky, and would not move—to my great disappointment; I wanted to prolong the pleasure of
success. What a glorious sensation it is to be for five
hours together winning—winning—winning! always
feeling what a whist player feels when he takes up four
honours, seven trumps! Who would think that a little
bit of leather, and two pieces of wood, had such a
delightful and delighting power!

The only drawback on my enjoyment was the failure

of the pretty boy, David Willis, who, injudiciously put in first, and playing for the first time in a match amongst men and strangers, who talked to him, and stared at him, was seized with such a fit of shame-faced shyness, that he could scarcely hold his bat, and was bowled out without a stroke, from actual nervousness. " He will come off that," Tom Coper says.—I am afraid he will. I wonder whether Tom had ever any modesty to lose. Our other modest lad, John Strong, did very well; his length told in fielding, and he got good fame. Joel Brent, the rescued mower, got into a scrape, and out of it again; his fortune for the day. He ran out his mate, Samuel Long; who, I do believe, but for the excess of Joel's eagerness, would have stayed in till this time, by which exploit he got into sad disgrace; and then he himself got thirty-seven runs, which redeemed his reputation. William Grey made a hit which actually lost the cricket ball. We think she lodged in a hedge, a quarter of a mile off, but nobody could find her. And George Simmons had nearly lost his shoe, which he tossed away in a passion, for having been caught out, owing to the ball glancing against it. These, together with a very complete somerset of Ben Appleton, our long-stop, who floundered about in the mud, making faces and attitudes as laughable as Grimaldi, none could tell whether by accident or design, were the chief incidents of the scene of action. Amongst the spectators nothing remarkable occurred, beyond the general calamity of two or three drenchings, except that a form, placed by the side of a hedge, under a very insufficient shelter, was knocked into the ditch, in a sudden rush of the cricketers to escape a pelting shower, by which means all parties shared the fate of Ben Appleton, some on land and some by water; and that, amidst the scramble, a saucy gipsy of a girl contrived to steal from the knee of the demure and well-apparelled Samuel Long, a smart handkerchief, which his careful dame had tied around it, to preserve his new (what is the mincing feminine word?)—his new—inexpressibles; thus reversing the story of Desdemona, and causing the new Othello to call aloud for his handkerchief, to the great diversion of the company.   And so we parted; the players retired to their supper, and we to our homes; all wet through, all good-humoured, and all happy—except the losers.

To-day we are happy too.   Hats, with ribands in them, go glancing up and down; and William Grey says, with a proud humility, " We do not challenge any parish; but if we be challenged, we are ready."

MARY RUSSELL MITFORD—*Our Village.*

RED *v.* BLACK

COMMONLY I rested an hour or two in the shade at noon, after planting, and ate my lunch, and read a little by a spring which was the source of a swamp and of a brook, oozing from under Brister's Hill, half a mile from my field. The approach to this was through a succession of descending grassy hollows, full of young pitch-pines, into a larger wood about the swamp. There, in a very secluded and shaded spot, under a spreading white-pine, there was yet a clean firm sward to sit on. I had dug out the spring, and made a well of clear grey water, where I could dip up a pailful without roiling it, and thither I went for this purpose almost every day in mid-summer, when the pond was warmest. Thither too the woodcock led her brood, to probe the mud for worms, flying but a foot above them down the bank, while they ran in a troop beneath; but at last, spying me, she would leave her young and circle round and round me, nearer and nearer till within four or five feet, pretending broken wings and legs, to attract my attention, and get off her young, who would already have taken up their march, with faint wiry peep, single file through the swamp, as she directed. Or I heard the peep of the young when I could not see the parent bird. There too the turtledoves sat over the spring, or fluttered from bough to bough of the soft white-pines over my head; or the red squirrel, coursing down the nearest bough, was particularly familiar and inquisitive. You only need sit still long enough in some attractive spot in the woods that all its inhabitants may exhibit themselves to you by turns.

I was witness to events of a less peaceful character. One day when I went out to my wood-pile, or rather my pile of stumps, I observed two large ants, the one red, the other much larger, nearly half an inch long, and black, fiercely contending with one another. Having once got hold they never let go, but struggled and wrestled and rolled on the chips incessantly. Looking farther, I was surprised to find that the chips were covered with such combatants, that it was not a *duellum*, but a *bellum*, a war between two races of ants, the red always pitted against the black, and frequently two red ones to one black. The legions of these Myrmidons covered all the hills and vales in my wood-yard, and the ground was already strewn with the dead and dying, both red and black. It was the only battle which I have ever witnessed, the only battle-field I ever trod while the battle was raging; internecine war; the red republicans on the one hand, and the black imperialists on the other. On every side they were engaged in deadly combat, yet without any noise that I could hear, and human soldiers never fought so resolutely. I watched a couple that were fast locked in each other's embraces, in a little sunny valley amid the chips, now at noon-day prepared to fight till the sun went down, or life went out. The smaller red champion had fastened himself like a vice to his adversary's front, and through all the tumblings on that field never for an instant ceased to gnaw at one of his feelers near the root, having already caused the other to go by the board; while the stronger black one dashed him from side to side, and, as I saw on looking nearer, had already divested him of several of his members. They fought with more pertinacity than bull-dogs. Neither manifested the least disposition to retreat. It was evident that their battle-cry was Conquer or die. In the meanwhile there came along a single red ant on the hill-side of this valley, evidently full of excitement, who either had despatched his foe, or had not yet taken part in the battle; probably the latter, for he had lost none of his limbs; whose mother had charged him to return with his shield or upon it. Or perchance he was some Achilles, who had nourished his wrath apart, and had now come to avenge or rescue his Patroclus. He saw this unequal combat from afar—for the blacks were nearly twice the size of the red—he drew near with rapid pace till he stood on his guard within half an inch of the combatants; then, watching his opportunity, he sprang upon the black warrior, and commenced his operations near the root of his right fore-leg, leaving the foe to select among his own members; and so there were three united for life, as if a new kind of attraction had been invented which put all other locks and cements to shame. I should not have wondered by this time to find that they had their respective musical bands stationed on some eminent chip, and playing their national airs the while, to excite the slow and cheer the dying combatants. I was myself excited somewhat even as if they had been men. The more you think of it, the less the difference. And certainly there is not a fight recorded in Concord history, at least, if in the history of America, that will bear a moment's comparison with this, whether for the numbers engaged in it, or for the patriotism and heroism displayed. For numbers and for carnage it was an Austerlitz or Dresden. Concord Fight! Two killed on the patriots' side, and Luther Blanchard wounded! Why, here every ant was a Buttrick,—" Fire! for God's sake, fire! "—and thousands shared the fate of Davis and Hosmer. There was not one hireling there. I have no doubt that it was a principle they fought for, as much as our ancestors, and not to avoid a threepenny tax on their tea; and the results of this battle will be as important and memorable to those whom it concerns as those of the battle of Bunker Hill, at least.

I took up the chip on which the three I have particularly described were struggling, carried it into my house, and placed it under a tumbler on my window-sill, in order to see the issue. Holding a microscope to the first mentioned red ant, I saw that, though he was assiduously gnawing at the near fore-leg of his enemy, having severed his remaining feeler, his own breast was all torn away, exposing what vitals he had there to the jaws of the black warrior, whose breast-plate was apparently too thick for him to pierce; and the dark carbuncles of the sufferer's eyes shone with ferocity such as war only could excite. They struggled half an hour longer under the tumbler, and when I looked again the black soldier had severed the heads of his foes from their bodies, and the still living heads were hanging on either side of him like ghastly trophies at his saddle bow, still apparently as firmly fastened as ever, and he was endeavouring with feeble struggles, being without feelers and with only the remnant of a leg, and I know not how many other wounds, to divest himself of them; which at length, after half an hour more, he accomplished. I raised the glass, and he went off over the window-sill in that crippled state. Whether he finally survived that combat, and spent the remainder of his days in some Hôtel des Invalides, I do not know; but I thought that his industry would not be worth much thereafter. I never learned which party was victorious, nor the cause of the war: but I felt for the rest of that day as if I had had my feelings excited and harrowed by witnessing the struggle, the ferocity and carnage, of a human battle before my door.

H. D. THOREAU—*Walden.* (*Brute Neighbours* [abridged]))

THE SEA-SERPENT

I have a confession to make, for I have it on my mind that I have done a very horrid thing. I am in doubt that I have committed the unpardonable sin, a sin than which there can be none more loathly—I believe that I have killed the sea-serpent, and that, too, ere he was fully grown. I will make you a full confession of it, and maybe it will ease the conscience that has to bear the weight of the accumulated doubt, and certainly of guilt.

It was not the only time that I had seen the sea-serpent. Once in the Banka Straits, in the days when I went to my islands, I leant upon the rail in company with another, who was shortly to be marooned, and the sea-serpent showed himself to us; knowing, I suppose, that we were about to leave the haunts of man, and could not tell his reality; trusting, I expect, to the sobering effects of isolation, which have till now forbade me abusing his confidence. I saw my companion with his eyes fixed upon it. I expected him to say, " Whatever is that? " and I thought that he only deserved the reply, " It is very long, it goes very fast; it is very big, and very much alive; but I don't know what it is." I fondly imagined that it would teach him caution, but presently,

97

D

after we had followed it with fascinated eyes, came the inevitable, " Do you think it might be the sea——? " " I told you I don't know what it is," and soon by good luck it was gone from sight. Beyond the exchange of a handshake, expressive of much trust and deep understanding, we showed the mocking world no sign.

Now that is true as I have told it, and to this day I do not know what that long live thing may have been. The Banka Straits would prove an ideal home for such as he: it is a place of swirls and eddies of mysterious water, where for a space the sea is smooth as glass, and for a space is tossed with white horses; where streaks like oil stretch through the waves as high-roads plain to see: a place of floating wrack, of slowly moving sea-snakes, of things that come quickly and as quickly go, and a place where dwells something very long, and very quickly moving.

Now to-day, after I have so long withstood the temptation of unveiling him, I come a-writing of him; and to-day I must unburden my conscience, for I believe that I have on my hands the blood of one of his children. That is my confession and the reason for laying bare my sins to you.

This time he came up out of thirteen hundred fathoms of dark blue water; came slowly to the surface sorely maimed, that once before he died he might show himself to doubting man. His home was in that deep trough of Indian Ocean that washes Sumbawa's southern shores; and twenty miles from land we were lying at the time of his visit. I left my fishing, where I tried with every art I knew to make a very large and very lazy shark take into his mouth many pounds of iron shaped hook-wise, and but ill-disguised by the presence of a dead duck and some bacon. I left the shark to himself and went to the bows of the ship, where the crowd of natives were watching the thing in all the wonder of its long body and gay colours. He had just come up out of the great deepness of those indigo transparencies, and he lay in the water, just keeping pace with the current that ran past our overhanging bows. The Malays stared at him, the Chinese gaped, and in truth he was a sight to make the breath come in gasps. A long silvery body, the one side reflecting the blue of deep ocean, the other the royal-mail red of the ship's boot-topping; a graceful ripple of the dorsal fin, crimson and delicate; and now and again the projection high above the water of the waving scarlet crest. Such was a first sight impression of him. Strange and beautiful he looked as I stared at him from above, something that man ought not to see, something to be spoken of only in hushed voices, something it were wrong to meddle with. And yet so little reverence has man for Nature's mysteries, that the next thing is the running for hooks and bait, and the vowing that by some means or other we must have him, must get him aboard and examine him. Someone looks for the harpoons, and cannot find them; another makes a running bowline to snare him with; I tempt him with a baited hook, which he ignores, and try to foul hook him with a bunch of shark hooks, which he does not heed. His only response to our best efforts is the slow elevation of the lovely scarlet crest, and its equally slow depression. For ever the ripple of scarlet shimmers down his length, and the blue and silver play alternate on his sides; for ever his mouth

opens and shuts with a steady rhythmic movement, as
he keeps his long body poised in the water. For ever
the strange scarlet crest goes slowly up and down, rising
and quivering against the current, standing in its full
dignity of two or three feet above the water, and then
slowly sinking back again.

For many crowded minutes he displays himself
suspended in the clear water, and then, turning slowly
on his side, shows the whole wealth of his silvery
splendour, looks at us with a great sad eye, twists supple
round our bows, and slowly sinks. We watch him as he
goes, his silver turned to blue, the blue to indigo, his
scarlet plume and crest lost in the very deepness of the
transparent water. Only a quiver of pink light or a
dazzle of silver shoots sideways as now and again he
slowly turns his body as he sinks. One thing we see as
he fades sadly from our sight, and it gives the clue to
the whole pathos of the scene—he has no tail. Somehow or other he has been cut off short. A shark or
some other monster has shorn him of his strength, and
instead of tantalizing us by swiftly skimming along the
surface of the water, as is his wont, he has come, feeling
death to be near, to give man the best view that he has
ever had of one of his race.

Slowly we realized it all, we had seen the last of him.
He had sunk to his cold and silent grave upon the ooze,
beneath all those thirteen hundred fathoms of blue
water, fearful lest man should find his remains and make
a boast of them. We have had our last look at the sea-
serpent, and now we can only talk of him—but at least
we can talk, now that he has gone, without lowering our
voices to a whisper. We are certain that none have seen

so clearly his like before, are sure that he was every inch
of twelve feet long, that the crest and plumes were something to be wondered at, and that the expression of his
eye was very, very sad.

Somehow there is something that is strangely familiar
in all this. The crested head that appeared above the
waves, the mane that marked the rising neck, and above
all the great pathetic eye; we knew them all. Never a
sailor's story of the sea-serpent, but the crest, the mane,
and the great sad eye were there—we had simply joined
the ranks of those who are branded with the brand of
Ananias—those who go down to the sea in ships and
see that great leviathan.

Well, he was gone, and it were wiser to forget him,
to pretend that he had never been; and I believe each
one of us resolved that nothing would ever make him
tell the tale to those who spend their lives at ease. Now
this, by every tradition of the sea, should be the end of
a sea-serpent story; all hands had seen him, his most
inconsiderable details had been noted; he had come with
dignity, and with dignity he had gone. But of my story
this is not the end, for I have yet my confession to
make.

Sadly I turned away from the bows to continue luring
the sharks that seemed so commonplace and vulgar by
comparison. But the sport had grown tame: the brown
and blunt-nosed things would circle round the hook,
eager for the bacon, dreading the barb, and even were
they hooked, where was the scarlet plume, where the
silver sheen, and what in those horrid grey eyes could
compare with the great pathetic ones that had so lately
looked up at me? Curiosity, and the backwardness of

the sharks, soon had me back a-gazing into the blue
depths in which I had seen the scarlet crest go down,
and even as I gazed, a glint of silver suddenly caught
told me that he was still near at hand. The silver
flashed again, and then a sidelong pink ripple, and there
was no doubt that he was coming up again.

A boat is lowered and manned, and it stands by in
readiness, hidden under the port side of the ship; the
long silver body comes nearer to the surface, and I take
my stand at the bows, with a double-barrel loaded with
number fours. Now some moments of suspense as he
stays poised uncertain whether to rise or sink, and then
up he comes, slowly and with infinite dignity. It is
clear to us all the reason for his return, for now he is
displaying two long and gaudy streamers that grow from
below his front fins. When first he came these were
pressed in close to his sides, and we had had no chance
to see them, and it was the doubt that we had not seen
all his beauty, when he sang his swan song to us, that
had brought him back again. He turns on his side that
we may see them float free of his silvery body, and his
head comes to the surface. The contents of the left
barrel goes in between his eyes, but the right barrel,
alas, shatters his wonderful crest. With the report the
boat starts off, but it is a long while before the Malays
can make the bows, and then the long body is drifting
fast astern a-down the starboard side, sinking, sinking,
ever sinking as it goes. Round the bows in a great curve
sweeps the boat, and all hands run aft along the deck,
shouting to the boatmen as a flash of silver reveals the
sinking body. By the time they are up to him he has
nearly gone astern, and he is in the water deep below

them. Then the unexpected thing happens, for he starts to rise again directly alongside the boat; a boat-hook helps him on, and with four pairs of arms around his silver girth he is hoisted inboard.

The sharks that have been dallying around my hook astern, realize that they have missed a victim, and all too late come upon the scene, with no more to be done than to follow the boat back to the ship. Now he is ours to do with as we will, we hoist him on deck and examine him, and find that though in truth we have got the sea-serpent, we have not got nearly all of him, for a great portion of his length must be a-missing. We measure him, and, mutilated as he is, he is only three inches short of twelve feet long. His crest is gone, but one scarlet streamer remains intact, and the crimson fin that runs the whole length of his back is there to see and wonder at.

He was ours to cut up and examine, and he was duly cut up and examined. Rude hands rubbed off, in sheer delight, the silver from his sides, and toyed with the strange mouth that was innocent of teeth. Rude hands carved him up to make shark bait, and the flesh was pink like that of salmon, but no man ate of it. It was to me a sign of his romantic origin, that no part of him, save his scarlet fin, would stand the wear and tear of human usage. Lest profane man would make a boast of his remains, should make a show of his carcass, he is composed of a substance entirely perishable; and his great body dissolved in sunshine as a dream will melt in waking. Save a sticky pinkish water, and a shine of silver, there is nothing of the sea-serpent that a man may keep for his reputation's sake; and who will believe that a man has slain the sea-serpent because he may treasure some sticky fluid and a little silver?

Now time alone has made me tell you this story, for I could no longer bear to keep to myself the secret of my crime. This is all true, that I slew the sea-serpent when he was not full grown, and when he was sorely maimed; and of all things that I have ever seen he was most like those made-up monsters that the Chinese love to carry in their New Year processions—even his silver was not stuck on tight, it could all be rubbed off, and his black spots looked unreal.

You may say that if this is true, why do I write of it thus, and why have I not told of it before. My excuse is that it is only my wish to confess that has made me break my silence now, and who would dare to tell with more authoritative note that he had killed a sea-serpent ere it was fully grown? No one might tell the world with serious intent that he had even seen him, no one would risk the infamy that would surely be his, did he say that he had fingered him, had rubbed off his silver, and opened his stomach to see upon what he fed.

I have handled the sea-serpent with familiarity, as the child, when picking up the shooting star, toyed with it till it was spoiled by the wearing away of its silver points; but the doing of it can bring no kudos to me. I would sooner say that I had not seen it than have the world suspect that I had thrown in my lot with the sailor-man. Only when I am asked what is the scarlet streamer which decorates my wall do I venture to own up; and then only if the questioner sits late into the night with me.

FREDERIC WOOD JONES—*Unscientific Essays.*

TRAVELLERS' TALES

My long residence here begins to fatigue me. As every object ceases to be new, it no longer continues to be pleasing; some minds are so fond of variety, that pleasure itself, if permanent, would be insupportable, and we are thus obliged to solicit new happiness even by courting distress. I only, therefore, wait the arrival of my son to vary this trifling scene, and borrow new pleasure from danger and fatigue. A life, I own, thus spent in wandering from place to place, is at best but empty dissipation. But to pursue trifles is the lot of humanity; and whether we bustle in a pantomime or strut at a coronation; whether we shout at a bonfire, or harangue in a senate house; whatever object we follow, it will at last surely conduct us to futility and disappointment. The wise bustle and laugh as they walk in the pageant, but fools bustle and are important; and this probably is all the difference between them.

This may be an apology for the levity of my former correspondence; I talked of trifles, and I knew that they were trifles; to make the things of this life ridiculous, it is only sufficient to call them by their names.

In other respects, I have omitted several striking circumstances in the description of this country, as

D*

supposing them either already known to you, or as not being thoroughly known to myself: but there is one omission for which I expect no forgiveness, namely, my being totally silent upon their buildings, roads, rivers and mountains. This is a branch of science on which all other travellers are so very prolix, that my deficiency will appear the more glaring. With what pleasure, for instance, do some read of a traveller in Egypt, measuring a fallen column with his cane, and finding it exactly five feet nine inches long; of his creeping through the mouth of a catacomb, and coming out by a different hole from that he entered; of his stealing the finger of an antique statue, in spite of the janizary that watched him; or his adding a new conjecture to the hundred and fourteen conjectures already published, upon the names of Osiris and Isis!

Methinks I hear some of my friends in China demanding a similar account of London and the adjacent villages; and if I remain here much longer, it is probable I may gratify their curiosity. I intend, when run dry on other topics, to take a serious survey of the city wall; to describe that beautiful building the mansion house; I will enumerate the magnificent squares in which the nobility chiefly reside, and the royal palaces appointed for the reception of the English monarch; nor will I forget the beauties of Shoe-lane, in which I myself have resided since my arrival. You shall find me no way inferior to many of my brother-travellers in the arts of description. At present, however, as a specimen of this way of writing, I send you a few hasty remarks, collected in a late journey I made to Kentish Town, and this in the manner of modern voyagers.

" Having heard much of Kentish Town, I conceived a strong desire to see that celebrated place. I could have wished, indeed, to satisfy my curiosity without going thither, but that was impracticable, and therefore I resolved to go. Travellers have two methods of going to Kentish Town; they take coach, which costs ninepence, or they may go a-foot, which costs nothing: in my opinion, a coach is by far the most eligible convenience, but I was resolved to go on foot, having considered with myself, that going in that manner would be the cheapest way.

" As you set out from Dog-house bar, you enter upon a fine level road railed in on both sides, commanding on the right a fine prospect of groves, and fields, enamelled with flowers, which would wonderfully charm the sense of smelling, were it not for a dunghill on the left, which mixes its effluvia with their odours. This dunghill is of much greater antiquity than the road; and I must not omit a piece of injustice I was going to commit upon this occasion. My indignation was levelled against the makers of the dunghill, for having brought it so near the road; whereas it should have fallen upon the makers of the road, for having brought that so near the dunghill.

" After proceeding in this manner for some time, a building, resembling somewhat a triumphal arch, salutes the traveller's view. This structure, however, is peculiar to this country, and vulgarly called a turnpike-gate: I could perceive a long inscription in large characters on the front, probably upon the occasion of some triumph, but, being in haste, I left it to be made out by some subsequent adventurer who may happen to travel this way; so, continuing my course to the west, I soon arrived at an unwalled town, called Islington.

"Islington is a pretty neat town, mostly built of brick, with a church and bells: it has a small lake, or rather pond in the midst, though at present very much neglected. I am told it is dry in summer: if this be the case, it can be no very proper receptacle for fish, of which the inhabitants themselves seem sensible, by bringing all that is eaten there from London.

"After having surveyed the curiosities of this fair and beautiful town, I proceeded forward, leaving a fair stone building, called the White Conduit House, on my right. Here the inhabitants of London often assemble to celebrate a feast of hot rolls and butter: seeing such numbers, each with their little tables before them, employed on this occasion, must, no doubt, be a very amusing sight to the looker-on, but still more so to those who perform in the solemnity.

"From hence I parted with reluctance to Pancras, as it is written, or Pancridge as it is pronounced; but which should be both pronounced and written *Pangrace*: this emendation I will venture *meo arbitrio*: Παν, in the Greek language, signifies *all*, which, added to the English word *grace*, maketh *all grace*, or *Pangrace;* and, indeed, this is a very proper appellation to a place of so much sanctity as Pangrace is universally esteemed. However this be, if you except the parish church and its fine bells, there is little in Pangrace worth the attention of the curious observer.

"From Pangrace to Kentish Town is an easy journey of one mile and a quarter: the road lies through a fine champaign country, well watered with beautiful drains.

and enamelled with flowers of all kinds, which might contribute to charm every sense, were it not that the odoriferous gales are often more impregnated with dust than perfume.

"As you enter Kentish Town, the eye is at once presented with the shops of artificers, such as venders of candles, small-coal and hair-brooms; there are also several august buildings of red brick, with numberless sign-posts, or rather pillars, in a peculiar order of architecture. I send you a drawing of several, *vide* A. B. C. This pretty town probably borrows its name from its vicinity to the county of Kent; and indeed it is not unnatural that it should, as there are only London and the adjacent villages that lie between them. Be this as it will, perceiving night approach, I made a hasty repast on roasted mutton, and a certain dried fruit called potatoes, resolving to protract my remarks upon my return: and this I would very willingly have done, but was prevented by a circumstance which, in truth, I had for some time foreseen, for night coming on, it was impossible to take a proper survey of the country, as I was obliged to return home in the dark."

OLIVER GOLDSMITH—*The Citizen of the World.*

THE CAT BY THE FIRE

A BLAZING fire, a warm rug, candles lit and curtains drawn, the kettle on for tea (nor do the " first circles " despise the preference of a kettle to an urn, as the third or fourth may do), and finally, the cat before you, attracting your attention—it is a scene which everybody likes unless he has a morbid aversion to cats; which is not common. There are some nice inquirers, it is true, who are apt to make uneasy comparisons of cats with dogs— to say they are not so loving, that they prefer the house to the man, etc. But agreeably to the good old maxim, that " comparisons are odious," our readers, we hope, will continue to like what is likeable from its inferiority to something else—a process by which we might ingeniously contrive to put soot into every dish that is set before us, and to reject one thing after another, till we were pleased with nothing. Here is a good fireside, and a cat to it; and it would be our own fault, if, in removing to another house and another fireside, we did not take care that the cat removed with us. Cats cannot look to the moving of goods as men do. If we would have creatures considerate towards us, we must be so towards them. It is not to be expected of everybody, quadruped or biped, that they should stick to us in spite of our want of merit, like a dog or a benevolent sage. Besides, stories have been told of cats very much to the credit of their benignity; such as their following a master about like a dog, waiting at a gentleman's door to thank him for some obligation overnight, etc. And our readers may remember the history of the famous Godolphin Arabian, upon whose grave a cat that had lived with him in the stable went and stretched itself and died.

The cat purrs, as if it applauded our consideration, and gently moves its tail. What an odd expression of the power to be irritable and the will to be pleased there is in its face, as it looks up at us! We must own, that we do not prefer a cat in the act of purring, or of looking in that manner. It reminds us of the sort of smile, or *simmer* (*simper* is too weak and fleeting a word) that is apt to be in the faces of irritable people when they are pleased to be in a state of satisfaction. We prefer, for a general expression, the cat in a quiet, unpretending state, and the human countenance with a look indicative of habitual grace and composure, as if it were not necessary to take any violent steps to prove its amiability —the " smile without a smile," as the poet beautifully calls it.

Furthermore (in order to get rid at once of all that may be objected to poor Pussy, as boys at school get down their bad dumpling as fast as possible before the meat comes), we own we have an objection to the way in which a cat sports with a mouse before she kills it, tossing and jerking it about like a ball, and letting it go, in order to pounce upon it with the greater relish. And yet what right have we to apply human measures of cruelty to the inferior reflectability of a cat? Perhaps she has no idea of the mouse's being alive, in the sense that we have—most likely she looks upon it as a pleasant movable toy, made to be eaten—a sort of lively pudding, that oddly jumps hither and thither. It would be hard to beat into the head of a country squire of the old class that there is any cruelty in hunting a hare; and most assuredly it would be still harder to beat mouse-sparing into the head of a cat. You might read the most pungent essay on the subject into her ear, and she would only sneeze at it.

As to the unnatural cruelties, which we sometimes read of, committed by cats upon their offspring, they are exceptions to the common and beautiful rules of nature, and accordingly we have nothing to do with them. They are traceable to some unnatural circumstances of breeding or position. Enormities as monstrous are to be found among human beings, and argue nothing against the general character of the species. Even dogs are not always immaculate; and sages have made slips. Dr. Franklin cut off his son with a shilling for differing with him in politics.

But cats resemble tigers? They are tigers in miniature? Well, and very pretty miniatures they are. And what has the tiger himself done, that he has not a right to eat his dinner as well as Jones? A tiger treats a man much as a cat does a mouse;—granted; but we have no reason to suppose that he is aware of the man's sufferings, or means anything but to satisfy his hunger; and what have the butcher and poulterer been about meanwhile? The tiger, it is true, lays about him a little superfluously sometimes, when he gets into a sheepfold, and kills more than he eats; but does not the Squire or the Marquis do pretty much like him in the month of September? Nay, do we not hear of venerable judges, that would not hurt a fly, going about in that refreshing month, seeking whom they may lame? See the effect of habit and education! And you can educate the tiger in no other way than by attending to his stomach. Fill that, and he will want no men to eat, probably not even to lame. On the other hand, deprive Jones of his dinner for a day or two, and see what a state he will be in, especially if he is by nature irascible. Nay, keep him from it for a half an hour, and observe the tiger propensities of his stomach and fingers—how worthy of killing he thinks the cook, and what boxes of the ear he feels inclined to give the footboy.

Animals, by the nature of things, in their present state, dispose of one another into their respective stomachs, without ill-will on any side. They keep down the several populations of their neighbours, till time may come when superfluous population of any kind need not exist, and predatory appearances may vanish from the earth, as the wolves have done from England. But whether they may or not is not a question by a hundred times so important to moral inquirers as into the possibilities of human education and the nonsense of ill-will. Show the nonentity of that, and we may all get our dinners as jovially as we can, sure of these three undoubted facts—that life is long, death short, and the world beautiful. And so we bring our thoughts back again to the fireside, and look at the cat.

Poor Pussy! she looks up at us again, as if she thanked us for those vindications of dinner; and symbolically gives a twist of a yawn and a lick to her whiskers. Now she proceeds to clean herself all over, having a just sense of the demands of her elegant person, beginning judiciously with her paws, and fetching amazing tongues at her hind-hips. Anon, she scratches her neck with a foot of rapid delight, leaning her head towards it, and shutting her eyes, half to accommodate the action of the skin, and half to enjoy the luxury. She then rewards her paws with a few more touches;—look at the action of her head and neck, how pleasing it is, the ears pointed forward, and the neck gently arching to and fro. Finally, she gives a sneeze, and another twist of mouth and whiskers, and then, curling her tail towards her front claws, settles herself on her hind-quarters, in an attitude of bland meditation.

What does she think of?—of her saucer of milk at breakfast? or of the thump she got yesterday in the kitchen for stealing the meat? or of her own meat, the Tartar's dish, noble horse-flesh? or of her friend the cat next door, the most impassioned of serenaders? or of her little ones, some of whom are now large, and all of them gone. Is *that* among her recollections when she looks pensive? Does she taste of the noble prerogative sorrows of man?

She is a sprightly cat, hardly past her youth; so, happening to move the fringe of the rug a little with our foot, she darts out a paw, and begins plucking it and inquiring into the matter, as if it were a challenge to play, or something lively enough to be eaten. What a graceful action of that foot of hers, between delicacy and petulance!—combining something of a thrust out, a beat, and a scratch. There seems even something of a

little bit of fear in it, as if just enough to provoke her
courage, and give her the excitement of a sense of
hazard. We remember being much amused with seeing
a kitten manifestly making a series of experiments upon
the patience of its mother, trying how far the latter
would put up with positive bites and thumps. The
kitten ran at her every moment, gave her a knock or a
bite of the tail; and then ran back again, to recommence
the assault. The mother sat looking at her, as if
betwixt tolerance and admiration, to see how far the
spirit of the family was inherited or improved by her
sprightly offspring. At length, however, the " little
Pickle " presumed too far, and the mother, lifting up
her paw, and meeting her at the very nick of the
moment, gave her one of the most unsophisticated boxes
of the ear we ever beheld. It sent her rolling half over
the room, and made her come to a most ludicrous pause,
with the oddest little look of premature and wincing
meditation.

That lapping of the milk out of the saucer is what
one's human thirst cannot sympathize with. It seems
as if there could be no satisfaction in such a series of
atoms of drink. Yet the saucer is soon emptied; and
there is a refreshment to one's ears in that sound of
plashing with which the action is accompanied, and
which seems indicative of a like comfort to Pussy's
mouth. Her tongue is thin, and can make a spoon of
itself. This, however, is common to other quadrupeds
with the cat, and does not, therefore, more particularly
belong to our feline consideration. Not so the electricity
of its coat, which gives out sparks under the hand; its
passion for the herb valerian (did the reader ever see

one roll in it? it is a mad sight) and other singular delicacies of nature, among which, perhaps, is to be reckoned its taste for fish, a creature with whose element it has so little to do, that it is supposed even to abhor it; though lately we read somewhere of a swimming cat, that used to fish for itself. And this reminds us of an exquisite anecdote of dear, dogmatic, diseased, thoughtful, surly, charitable Johnson, who would go out of doors himself, and buy oysters for his cat, because his black servant was too proud to do it! Not that we condemn the black, in those enslaving unliberating days. He had a right to the mistake, though we should have thought better of him had he seen farther, and subjected his pride to affection for such a master. But Johnson's true practical delicacy in the matter is beautiful. Be assured that he thought nothing of " condescension " in it, or being eccentric. He was singular in some things, because he could not help it. But he hated eccentricity. No: in his best moments he felt himself simply to be a man, and a good man too, though a frail —one that in virtue as well as humility, and in a knowledge of his ignorance as well as his wisdom, was desirous of being a Christian philosopher; and accordingly he went out, and bought food for his hungry cat, because his poor negro was too proud to do it, and there was nobody else in the way whom he had a right to ask. What must anybody that saw him have thought as he turned up Bolt Court! But doubtless he went as secretly as possible—that is to say, if he considered the thing at all. His friend Garrick could not have done as much! He was too grand, and on the great " stage " of life. Goldsmith could; but he would hardly have thought of it. Beauclerc might; but he would have thought it necessary to excuse it with a jest or a wager, or some such thing. Sir Joshua Reynolds, with his fashionable, fine-lady-painting hand, would certainly have shrunk from it. Burke would have reasoned himself into its propriety, but he would have reasoned himself out again. Gibbon! Imagine its being put into the head of Gibbon!! He and his bag-wig would have started with all the horror of a gentleman-usher; and he would have rung the bell for the cook's-deputy's-under-assistant-errand-boy.

Cats at firesides live luxuriously, and are the picture of comfort; but lest they should not bear their portion of trouble in this world, they have the drawbacks of being liable to be shut out of doors on cold nights, beatings from the " aggravated " cooks, overpettings of children (how should we like to be squeezed and pulled about in that manner by some great patronizing giants?) and last, not least, horrible merciless tramples of unconscious human feet and unfeeling legs of chairs. Elegance, comfort and security seem the order of the day on all sides, and you are going to sit down to dinner, or to music, or to take tea, when all of a sudden the cat gives a squall as if she was mashed; and you are not sure that the fact is otherwise. Yet she gets in the way again, as before; and dares all the feet and mahogany in the room. Beautiful present sufficingness of a cat's imagination! Confined to the snug circle of her own sides, and the two next inches of rug or carpet.

Leigh Hunt—*Essays*.

TOBY

Toby was the most utterly shabby, vulgar, mean-looking cur I ever beheld: in one word, *a tyke*. He had not one good feature except his teeth and eyes, and his bark, if that can be called a feature. He was not ugly enough to be interesting; his colour black and white, his shape leggy and clumsy; altogether what Sydney Smith would have called an extraordinarily ordinary dog: and, as I have said, not even greatly ugly, or, as the Aberdonians have it, *bonnie wi' ill-fauredness*. My brother William found him the centre of attraction to a multitude of small blackguards who were drowning him slowly in Lochend Loch, doing their best to lengthen out the process, and secure the greatest amount of fun with the nearest approach to death. Even then Toby showed his great intellect by pretending to be dead, and thus gaining time and an inspiration. William bought him for twopence, and as he had it not, the boys accompanied him to Pilrig Street, when I happened to meet him, and giving the twopence to the biggest boy, had the satisfaction of seeing a general engagement of much severity, during which the twopence disappeared; one penny going off with a very small and swift boy, and the other vanishing hopelessly into the grating of a drain.

Toby was for weeks in the house unbeknown to anyone but ourselves two and the cook, and from my grandmother's love of tidiness and hatred of dogs and of dirt,
I believe she would have expelled " him whom we saved
from drowning " had not he, in his straightforward way,
walked into my father's bedroom one night when he
was bathing his feet, and introduced himself with a wag
of his tail, intimating a general willingness to be happy.
My father laughed most heartily, and at last Toby,
having got his way to his bare feet, and having begun
to lick his soles and between his toes with his small
rough tongue, my father gave such an unwonted shout
of laughter, that we—grandmother, sisters, and all of us
—went in. Grandmother might argue with all her
energy and skill, but as surely as the pressure of Tom
Jones's infantile fist upon Mr. Allworthy's forefinger
undid all the arguments of his sister, so did Toby's
tongue and fun prove too many for grandmother's
eloquence. I somehow think Toby must have been up
to all this, for I think he had a peculiar love for my
father ever after, and regarded grandmother from that
hour with a careful and cool eye.

Toby, when full grown, was a strong, coarse dog:
coarse in shape, in countenance, in hair, and in manner.
I used to think that, according to the Pythagorean
doctrine, he must have been, or been going to be, a
Gilmerton carter. He was of the bull-terrier variety,
coarsened through much mongrelism and a dubious
and varied ancestry. His teeth were good, and he had
a large skull, and a rich bark as of a dog three times
his size, and a tail which I never saw equalled—indeed
it was a tail *per se*; it was of immense girth and not

short, equal throughout like a policeman's baton; the machinery for working it was of great power, and acted in a way, as far as I have been able to discover, quite original. We called it his ruler.

When he wished to get into the house, he first whined gently, then growled, then gave a sharp bark, and then came a resounding, mighty stroke which shook the house; this, after much study and watching, we found was done by his bringing the entire length of his solid tail flat upon the door, with a sudden and vigorous stroke; it was quite a *tour de force* or a *coup de queue*, and he was perfect in it at once, his first *bang* authoritative, having been as masterly and telling as his last.

With all this inbred vulgar air, he was a dog of great moral excellence—affectionate, faithful, honest up to his light, with an odd humour as peculiar and as strong as his tail. My father, in his reserved way, was very fond of him, and there must have been very funny scenes with them, for we heard bursts of laughter issuing from his study when they two were by themselves: there was something in him that took that grave, beautiful, melancholy face. One can fancy him in the midst of his books, and sacred work and thoughts, pausing and looking at the secular Toby, who was looking out for a smile to begin his rough fun, and about to end by coursing and *gurrin'* round the room, upsetting my father's books, laid out on the floor for consultation, and himself nearly at times, as he stood watching him—and off his guard and shaking with laughter. Toby had always a great desire to accompany my father up to town; this my father's good taste and sense of dignity, besides his fear of losing his friend (a vain fear!), forbade, and as the decision of character of each was great and nearly equal, it was often a drawn game. Toby, ultimately, by making it his entire object, triumphed. He usually was nowhere to be seen on my father leaving; he however saw him, and lay in wait at the head of the street, and up Leith Walk he kept him in view from the opposite side like a detective, and then, when he knew it was hopeless to hound him home, he crossed unblushingly over, and joined company, excessively rejoiced of course.

One Sunday he had gone with him to church, and left him at the vestry door. The second psalm was given out, and my father was sitting back in the pulpit, when the door at its back, up which he came from the vestry, was seen to move, and gently open, then, after a long pause, a black shining snout pushed its way steadily into the congregation, and was followed by Toby's entire body. He looked somewhat abashed, but snuffing his friend, he advanced as if on thin ice, and not seeing him, put his fore-legs on the pulpit, and, behold, there he was, his own familiar chum. I watched all this, and anything more beautiful than his look of happiness, of comfort, of entire ease when he beheld his friend—the smoothing down of the anxious ears, the swing of gladness of that mighty tail—I don't expect soon to see. My father quietly opened the door, and Toby was at his feet invisible to all but himself: had he sent old George Peaston, the "minister's man," to put him out, Toby would probably have shown his teeth, and astonished George. He slunk home as soon as he could, and never repeated that exploit.

I never saw in any other dog the sudden transition from discretion, not to say abject cowardice, to blazing and permanent valour. From his earliest years he showed a general meanness of blood, inherited from many generations of starved, bekicked, and down-trodden forefathers and mothers, resulting in a condition of intense abjectness in all matters of personal fear; anybody, even a beggar, by a *gowl* and a threat of eye, could send him off howling by anticipation, with that mighty tail between his legs. But it was not always so to be, and I had the privilege of seeing courage, reasonable, absolute, and for life, spring up in Toby at once, as did Athene from the skull of Jove. It happened thus:

Toby was in the way of hiding his culinary bones in the small gardens before his own and the neighbouring doors. Mr. Scrymgeour, two doors off, a bulky, choleric, red-haired, red-faced man—*torvo voltu*—was, by law of contrast, a great cultivator of flowers, and he had often scowled Toby into all but non-existence by a stamp of his foot and a glare of his eye. One day his gate being open, in walks Toby with a huge bone, and making a hole where Scrymgeour had two minutes before been planting some precious slips, the name of which on paper and on a stick Toby made very light of, substituted his bone, and was engaged covering it, or thinking he was covering it up with his shovelling nose (a very odd relic of paradise in the dog), when Scrymgeour spied him through the inner glass-door, and was out upon him like the Assyrian, with a terrific *gowl*. I watched them. Instantly Toby made straight at him with a roar too, and an eye more torve than Scrymgeour's, who, retreating without reserve, fell prostrate, there is reason to believe, in his own lobby. Toby contented himself with proclaiming his victory at the door, and returning, finished his bone-planting at his leisure; the enemy, who had scuttled behind the glass-door, glaring at him.

From this moment Toby was an altered dog. Pluck at first sight was lord of all; from that time dated his first tremendous deliverance of tail against the door, which we called " come listen to my tail." That very evening he paid a visit to Leo, next door's dog, a big, tyrannical bully and coward, which its master thought a Newfoundland, but whose pedigree we knew better; this brute continued the same system of chronic exter-mination which was interrupted at Lochend—having Toby down among his feet, and threatening him with instant death two or three times a day. To him Toby paid a visit that very evening, down into his den, and walked about, as much as to say, " Come on, Macduff! " but Macduff did not come on and henceforward there was an armed neutrality, and they merely stiffened up and made their backs rigid, pretended each not to see the other, walking solemnly round, as is the manner of dogs. Toby worked his new-found faculty thoroughly, but with discretion. He killed cats, astonished beggars, kept his own in his own garden against all comers and came off victorious in several well-fought battles; but he was not quarrelsome or foolhardy. It was very odd how his carriage changed, holding his head up, and how much pleasanter he was at home. To my father, next to William, who was his Humane Society man, he remained staunch. He had a great dislike to all things abnormal, as the phrase now is. A young lady of his acquaintance was calling one day, and relating some distressing events, she became hysterical. Of this Toby did not approve, and sallying from under my father's chair, attacked his friend, barking fiercely, and cut short the hysterics better than any *sal volatile* or valerian. He then made abject apologies to the patient, and slunk back to his chair.

And what of his end? for the misery of dogs is that they die so soon, or, as Sir Walter says, it is well they do; for if they lived as long as a Christian, and we liked them in proportion, and they then died, he said that was a thing he could not stand.

His exit was lamentable, and had a strange poetic or tragic relation to his entrance. My father was out of town; I was away in England. Whether it was that the absence of my father had relaxed his power of moral restraint, or whether through neglect of the servant he had been desperately hungry, or most likely both being true, Toby was discovered with the remains of a cold leg of mutton, on which he had made an ample meal; this he was in vain endeavouring to plant as of old, in the hope of its remaining undiscovered till to-morrow's hunger returned, the whole shank-bone sticking up unmistakably. This was seen by our excellent and Rhadamanthine grandmother, who pronounced sentence on the instant; and next day, as William was leaving for the High School, did he in the sour morning, through an easterly *haur*, behold him " whom he saved from drowning," and whom, with better results than in the case of Launce and Crab, he had taught, as if one should say " thus would I teach a dog," dangling by his own chain from his own lamp-post, one of his hind feet just touching the pavement, and his body preternaturally elongated.

William found him dead and warm, and falling in with the milk-boy at the head of the street, questioned him, and discovered that he was the executioner, and had got twopence, he—Toby's every morning's crony, who met him and accompanied him up the street, and licked the outside of his can—had with an eye to speed and convenience, and a want of taste, not to say principle and affection, horrible still to think of, suspended Toby's animation beyond all hope. William instantly fell upon him, upsetting his milk and cream, and gave him a thorough licking, to his own intense relief; and, being late, he got from Pyper, who was a martinet, the customary palmies, which he bore with something approaching to pleasure. So died Toby: my father said little, but he missed and mourned his friend.

There is reason to believe that by one of those curious intertwistings of existence, the milk-boy was that one of the drowning party who got the penny of the two-pence.

DR. JOHN BROWN—*Our Dogs.*

THE CHARACTER OF AN IMPORTANT
TRIFLER

Though naturally pensive, yet I am fond of gay company, and take every opportunity of thus dismissing the mind from duty. From this motive, I am often found in the centre of a crowd; and wherever pleasure is to be sold, am always a purchaser. In those places, without being remarked by any, I join in whatever goes forward; work my passions into a similitude of frivolous earnestness, shout as they shout, and condemn as they happen to disapprove. A mind thus sunk for a while below its natural standard, is qualified for stronger flights, as those first retire who would spring forward with greater vigour.

Attracted by the serenity of the evening, my friend and I lately went to gaze upon the company in one of the public walks near the city. Here we sauntered together for some time, either praising the beauty of such as were handsome, or the dresses of such as had nothing else to recommend them. We had gone thus deliberately forward for some time, when, stopping on a sudden, my friend caught me by the elbow, and led me out of the public walk. I could perceive by the quickness of his pace, and by his frequently looking behind, that he was attempting to avoid somebody who followed: we now turned to the right, then to the left, as we went forward he still went faster, but in vain; the person whom he attempted to escape hunted us through every doubling, and gained upon us each moment: so that at last we fairly stood still, resolving to face what we could not avoid.

Our pursuer soon came up, and joined us with all the familiarity of an old acquaintance. My dear Drybone, cries he, shaking my friend's hand, where have you been hiding this half a century? Positively I had fancied you were gone to cultivate matrimony and your estate in the country. During the reply, I had an opportunity of surveying the appearance of our new companion: his hat was pinched up with peculiar smartness; his looks were pale, thin and sharp; round his neck he wore a broad black riband, and in his bosom a buckle studded with glass; his coat was trimmed with tarnished twist; he wore by his side a sword with a black hilt; and his stockings of silk, though newly washed, were grown yellow by long service. I was so much engaged with the peculiarity of his dress, that I attended only to the latter part of my friend's reply, in which he complimented Mr. Tibbs on the taste of his clothes, and the bloom in his countenance: Pshaw, pshaw, Will, cried the figure, no more of that, if you love me: you know I hate flattery, on my soul I do; and yet, to be sure, an intimacy with the great will improve one's appearance, and a course of venison will fatten; and yet, faith, I despise the great as much as you do: but there are a great many honest fellows among them; and we must not quarrel with one half, because the other wants weeding. If they were all such as my Lord Mudler, one of the most good-natured creatures that ever squeezed a lemon, I should myself be among the number of their admirers. I was yesterday to dine at the Duchess of Piccadilly's. My lord was there. Ned, says he to me, Ned, says he, I'll hold gold to silver, I can tell where you were poaching last night.

Ah, Tibbs, thou art a happy fellow, cried my companion, with looks of infinite pity; I hope your fortune is as much improved as your understanding in such company? Improved, replied the other; you shall know—but let it go no farther—a great secret—five hundred a year to begin with.—My lord's word of honour for it—his lordship took me down in his own chariot yesterday, and we had a *tête-à-tête* dinner in the country, where we talked of nothing else. I fancy you forget, sir, cried I, you told us but this moment of your dining yesterday in town. Did I say so? replied he coolly; to be sure if I said so, it was so—dined in town: egad, now I do remember, I did dine in town: but I dined in the country too; for you must know, my boys, I eat two dinners. By the bye, I am grown as nice as the devil in my eating. I'll tell you a pleasant affair about that: We were a select party of us to dine at Lady Grogram's, an affected piece, but let it go no farther; a secret: well, there happened to be no assafœtida in the sauce to a turkey, upon which, says I, I'll hold a thousand guineas, and say, done first, that—but dear Drybone, you are an honest creature, lend me half a crown for a minute or two, or so, just till—but hearkee, ask me for it the next time we meet, or it may be twenty to one but I forget to pay you.

When he left us, our conversation naturally turned

upon so extraordinary a character. His very dress, cries my friend, is not less extraordinary than his conduct. If you meet him this day, you find him in rags; if the next, in embroidery. With those persons of distinction of whom he talks so familiarly, he has scarcely a coffee-house acquaintance. However, both for the interests of society, and perhaps for his own, heaven has made him poor, and while all the world perceive his wants, he fancies them concealed from every eye. An agreeable companion, because he understands flattery; and all must be pleased with the first part of his conversation, though all are sure of its ending with a demand on their purse. While his youth countenances the levity of his conduct, he may thus earn a precarious subsistence: but when age comes on, the gravity of which is incompatible with buffoonery, then will he find himself forsaken by all; condemned in the decline of life to hang upon some rich family whom he once despised, there to undergo all the ingenuity of studied contempt, to be employed only as a spy upon the servants, or a bugbear to fright the children into obedience.

OLIVER GOLDSMITH—*The Citizen of the World.*

E

GIPSIES

As I was yesterday riding out in the fields with my friend
Sir Roger, we saw at a little distance from us a troop of
gipsies. Upon the first discovery of them, my friend was
in some doubt whether he should not exert the justice of
peace upon such a band of lawless vagrants: but not
having his clerk with him, who is a necessary counsellor
on these occasions, and fearing that his poultry might
fare the worse for it, he let the thought drop: but at the
same time gave me a particular account of the mischiefs
they do in the country, in stealing people's goods, and
spoiling their servants. "If a stray piece of linen hangs
upon an hedge," says Sir Roger, "they are sure to have
it; if a hog loses his way in the fields, it is ten to one
but he becomes their prey: our geese cannot live in
peace for them. If a man prosecutes them with severity,
his hen-roost is sure to pay for it. They generally
straggle into these parts about this time of the year; and
set the heads of our servant-maids so agog for husbands,
that we do not expect to have any business done as it
should be, whilst they are in the country. I have an
honest dairy-maid who crosses their hands with a piece
of silver every summer, and never fails being promised
the handsomest young fellow in the parish for her pains.

Your friend the butler has been fool enough to be seduced by them; and though he is sure to lose a knife, a fork, or a spoon every time his fortune is told him, generally shuts himself up in the pantry with an old gipsy for about half an hour once in a twelvemonth. Sweethearts are the things they live upon, which they bestow very plentifully upon all those that apply themselves to them."

Sir Roger, observing that I listened with great attention to his account of a people who were so entirely new to me, told me, that if I would, they should tell us our fortunes. As I was very well pleased with the knight's proposal, we rid up and communicated our hands to them. A Cassandra of the crew, after having examined my lines very diligently, told me that I loved a pretty maid in a corner, that I was a good woman's man, with some other particulars, which I do not think proper to relate. My friend Sir Roger alighted from his horse, and exposing his palm to two or three that stood by him, they crumpled it into all shapes, and diligently scanned every wrinkle that could be made in it; when one of them, who was older and more sunburnt than the rest, told him that he had a widow in his line of life. Upon which the knight cried, " Go, go, you are an idle baggage "; and at the same time smiled upon me. The gipsy, finding he was not displeased in his heart, told him, after a farther inquiry into his hand, that his true love was constant, and that she should dream of him to-night. My old friend cried Pish, and bid her go on. The gipsy told him that he was a bachelor, but would not be so long; and that he was dearer to somebody than he thought. The knight still repeated, " She was an

idle baggage," and bid her go on. " Ah, master,"
says the gipsy, " that roguish leer of yours makes a
pretty woman's heart ache; you have not that simper
about the mouth for nothing." The uncouth gibberish
with which all this was uttered, like the darkness of an
oracle, made us the more attentive to it. To be
short, the knight left the money with her that he had
crossed her hand with, and got up again on his
horse.

As we were riding away, Sir Roger told me that he
knew several sensible people who believed these gipsies
now and then foretold very strange things; and for half
an hour together appeared more jocund than ordinary.
In the height of this good humour, meeting a common
beggar upon the road, who was no conjurer, as he went
to relieve him, he found his pocket was picked: that
being a kind of palmistry at which this race of vermin
are very dexterous.

I might here entertain my reader with historical
remarks on this idle, profligate people, who infest all the
countries of Europe, and live in the midst of govern-
ments in a kind of commonwealth by themselves. But,
instead of entering into observations of this nature, I
shall fill the remaining part of my paper with a story
which is still fresh in Holland, and was printed in one
of our monthly accounts about twenty years ago. " As
the *trekschuyt*, or hackney-boat, which carries passengers
from Leyden to Amsterdam, was putting off, a boy running along the side of the canal desired to be taken in;
which the master of the boat refused because the lad
had not quite money enough to pay the usual fare. An
eminent merchant being pleased with the looks of the

boy, and secretly touched with compassion towards him, paid the money for him, and ordered him to be taken on board. Upon talking with him afterwards, he found that he could speak readily in three or four languages, and learned, upon further examination, that he had been stolen away when he was a child by a gipsy, and had rambled ever since with a gang of those strollers up and down several parts of Europe. It happened that the merchant, whose heart seems to have inclined towards the boy by a secret kind of instinct, had himself lost a child some years before. The parents, after a long search for him, gave him for drowned in one of the canals with which that country abounds; and the mother was so afflicted at the loss of a fine boy, who was her only son, that she died for grief of it. Upon laying together all particulars, and examining the several moles and marks by which the mother used to describe the child when he was first missing, the boy proved to be the son of the merchant, whose heart had so unaccountably melted at the sight of him. The lad was very well pleased to find a father who was so rich, and likely to leave him a good estate: the father, on the other hand, was not a little delighted to see a son return to him, whom he had given for lost, with such a strength of constitution, sharpness of understanding, and skill in languages." Here the printed story leaves off; but if I may give credit to reports, our linguist having received such extraordinary rudiments towards a good education, was afterwards trained up in everything that becomes a gentleman; wearing off, by little and little, all the vicious habits and practices that he had been used to in the course of his peregrinations. Nay, it is said that he has since been employed in foreign courts upon national business, with great reputation to himself, and honour to those who sent him, and that he has visited several countries as a public minister, in which he formerly wandered as a gipsy.

JOSEPH ADDISON—*The Spectator.*

A LAZY IDLE BOY

I HAD occasion to pass a week in the autumn in the little old town of Coire or Chur, in the Grisons, where lies buried that very ancient British king, saint, and martyr, Lucius, who founded the Church of St. Peter, which stands opposite the house No. 65 Cornhill. Few people note the church nowadays, and fewer ever heard of the saint. In the cathedral at Chur, his statue appears surrounded by other sainted persons of his family. With tight red breeches, a Roman habit, a curly brown beard, and a neat little gilt crown and sceptre, he stands, a very comely and cheerful image: and, from what I may call his peculiar position with regard to No. 65 Cornhill, I beheld this figure of St. Lucius with more interest than I should have bestowed upon personages who, hierarchically, are, I dare say, his superiors.

The pretty little city stands, so to speak, at the end of the world—of the world of to-day, the world of rapid motion, and rushing railways, and the commerce and intercourse of men. From the northern gate, the iron road stretches away to Zürich, to Basel, to Paris, to home. From the old southern barriers, before which a little river rushes, and around which stretch the crumbling battlements of the ancient town, the road bears the slow diligence or lagging vetturino by the shallow Rhine, through the awful gorges of the Via Mala, and presently over the Splügen to the shores of Como.

I have seldom seen a place more quaint, pretty, calm and pastoral than this remote little Chur. What need have the inhabitants for walls and ramparts, except to build summer-houses, to trail vines, and hang clothes to dry? No enemies approach the great mouldering gates: only at morn and even, the cows come lowing past them, the village maidens chatter merrily round the fountains, and babble like the ever-voluble stream that flows under the old walls. The schoolboys, with book and satchel, in smart uniform, march up to the gymnasium, and return thence at their stated time. There is one coffee-house in the town, and I see one old gentleman goes to it. There are shops with no customers seemingly, and the lazy tradesmen look out of their little windows at the single strangers sauntering by. There is a stall with baskets of queer little black grapes and apples, and a pretty brisk trade with half a dozen urchins standing round. But, beyond this, there is scarce any talk or movement in the street. There's nobody at the book-shop. "If you will have the goodness to come again in an hour," says the banker, with his mouth full of dinner at one o'clock, "you can have the money." There is nobody at the hotel, save the good landlady, the kind waiters, the brisk young cook who ministers to you. Nobody is in the Protestant church—(oh! strange sight, the two confessions are here at peace!)—nobody in the Catholic church: until the sacristan, from his snug abode in the cathedral close, espies the traveller eyeing the monsters and pillars before the old shark-toothed arch of his cathedral, and comes out (with a view to remuneration possibly) and opens the gate, and shows you the venerable church, and the queer old relics in the sacristy, and the ancient vestments (a black velvet cope, amongst other robes, as fresh as yesterday, and presented by that notorious " pervert," Henry of Navarre and France), and the statue of St. Lucius, who built St. Peter's Church, opposite No. 65 Cornhill.

What a quiet, kind, quaint, pleasant, pretty old town! Has it been asleep these hundreds and hundreds of years, and is the brisk young Prince of the Sidereal Realms in his screaming car drawn by his snorting steel elephant coming to waken it? Time was when there must have been life and bustle and commerce here. Those vast, venerable walls were not made to keep out cows, but men-at-arms led by fierce captains, who prowled about the gates, and robbed the traders as they passed in and out with their bales, their goods, their pack-horses, and their wains. Is the place so dead that even the clergy of the different denominations can't quarrel? Why, seven or eight, or a dozen, or fifteen hundred years ago (they haven't the register, over the way, up to that remote period. I dare say it was burnt in the Fire of London)—a dozen hundred years ago, when there was some life in the town, St. Lucius was stoned here on account of theological differences, after founding our church in Cornhill.

There was a sweet pretty river walk we used to take in the evening; and mark the mountains round glooming with a deeper purple; the shades creeping up the golden walls; the river brawling, the cattle calling, the maids and chatterboxes round the fountains babbling and

E*

bawling; and several times in the course of our sober walks, we overtook a lazy slouching boy, or hobbledehoy, with a rusty coat, and trousers not too long, and big feet trailing lazily one after the other, and large lazy hands dawdling from out the tight sleeves, and in the lazy hands a little book, which my lad held up to his face, and which I dare say so charmed and ravished him, that he was blind to the beautiful sights around him; unmindful, I would venture to lay any wager, of the lessons he had to learn for to-morrow; forgetful of mother waiting supper, and father preparing a scolding; absorbed utterly and entirely in his book.

What was it that so fascinated the young student, as he stood by the river shore? Not the *Pons Asinorum*. What book so delighted him, and blinded him to all the rest of the world, so that he did not care to see the apple-woman with her fruit, or (more tempting still to sons of Eve) the pretty girls with their apple cheeks, who laughed and prattled round the fountain? What was the book? Do you suppose it was Livy, or the Greek grammar? No; it was a NOVEL that you were reading, you lazy, not very clean, good-for-nothing, sensible boy! It was D'Artagnan locking up General Monk in a box, or almost succeeding in keeping Charles the First's head on. It was the prisoner of the Château d'If cutting himself out of the sack fifty feet under water (I mention the novels I like best myself—novels without love or talking, or any of that sort of nonsense, but containing plenty of fighting, escaping, robbery and rescuing)—cutting himself out of the sack, and swimming to the Island of Monte Cristo. O Dumas! O thou brave, kind, gallant old Alexandre! I hereby offer thee homage, and give thee thanks for many pleasant hours. I have read thee (being sick in bed) for thirteen hours of a happy day, and had the ladies of the house fighting for the volumes. Be assured that lazy boy was reading Dumas (or I will go so far as to let the reader here pronounce the eulogium, or insert the name of his favourite author); and as for the anger, or it may be, the reverberations of his schoolmaster, or the remonstrances of his father, or the tender pleadings of his mother that he should not let the supper grow cold—I don't believe the scapegrace cared one fig. No! Figs are sweet, but fictions are sweeter.

Have you ever seen a score of white-bearded, white-robed warriors, or grave seniors of the city, seated at the gate of Jaffa or Beyrout, and listening to the story-teller reciting his marvels out of *Antar* or the *Arabian Nights*? I was once present when a young gentleman at table put a tart away from him, and said to his neighbour, the Younger Son (with rather a fatuous air), "I never eat sweets."

"Not eat sweets! and do you know why?" says T.

"Because I am past that kind of thing," says the young gentleman.

"Because you are a glutton and a sot!" cries the elder (and Juvenis winces a little). "All people who have natural, healthy appetites love sweets; all children, all women, all Eastern people, whose tastes are not corrupted by gluttony and strong drink." And a plateful of raspberries and cream disappeared before the philosopher.

You take the allegory? Novels are sweets. All people with healthy literary appetites love them—almost all women;—a vast number of clever, hard-headed men. Why, one of the most learned physicians in England said to me only yesterday, " I have just read *So-and-So* for the second time " (naming one of Jones's exquisite fictions). Judges, bishops, chancellors, mathematicians are notorious novel-readers; as well as young boys and sweet girls, and their kind, tender mothers. Who has not read about Eldon, and how he cried over novels every night when he was not at whist?

As for that lazy, naughty boy at Chur, I doubt whether *he* will like novels when he is thirty years of age. He is taking too great a glut of them now. He is eating jelly until he will be sick. He will know most plots by the time he is twenty, so that *he* will never be surprised when the Stranger turns out to be the rightful earl— when the old Waterman, throwing off his beggarly gabardine, shows his stars and the collars of his various orders, and clasping Antonia to his bosom, proves himself to be the prince, her long-lost father. He will recognize the novelists' same characters, though they appear in red-heeled pumps and *ailes-de-pigeon*, or the garb of the nineteenth century. He will get weary of sweets, as boys of private schools grow (or used to grow, for I have done growing some little time myself, and the practice may have ended too)—as private schoolboys used to grow tired of the pudding before their mutton at dinner.

And pray what is the moral of this apologue? The moral I take to be this: the appetite for novels extending to the end of the world;—far away in the frozen deep, the sailors reading them to one another during the endless night;—far away under the Syrian stars, the solemn sheikhs and elders hearkening to the poet as he recites his tales;—far away in the Indian camps, where the soldiers listen to ——'s tales, or ——'s, after the hot day's march;—far away in little Chur yonder, where the lazy boy pores over the fond volume, and drinks it in with all his eyes;—the demand being what we know it is, the merchant must supply it, as he will supply saddles and pale ale for Bombay or Calcutta.

But as surely as the cadet drinks too much pale ale, it will disagree with him; and so surely, dear youth, will too much novels cloy on thee.

W. M. THACKERAY—*Roundabout Papers.*

FEBRUARY DAYS

THE snow has gone from the landscape and the sun, at the hour of setting, has got round to the wood that crowns the hill on the other side of the valley. Soon it will set on the slope of the hill and then down on the plain. Then we shall know that spring has come. Two days ago a blackbird, from the paddock below the orchard, added his golden baritone to the tenor of the thrush who had been shouting good news from the beech tree across the road for weeks past. I don't know why the thrush should glimpse the dawn of the year before the blackbird, unless it is that his habit of choosing the topmost branches of the tree gives him a better view of the world than that which the golden-throated fellow gets on the lower branches that he always affects. It may be the same habit of living in the top storey that accounts for the early activity of the rooks. They are noisy neighbours, but never so noisy as in these late February days, when they are breaking up into families and quarrelling over their slatternly household arrangements in the topmost branches of the elm trees. They are comic ruffians who wash all their dirty linen in public, and seem almost as disorderly and bad-tempered as the human family itself. If they had only a little of our ingenuity in mutual slaughter there would be no need for my friend the farmer to light bonfires underneath the trees in order to drive the female from the eggs and save his crops.

A much more amiable little fellow, the great tit, has just added his modest assurance that spring is coming. He is not much of a singer, but he is good hearing to anyone whose thoughts are turning to his garden and the pests that lurk therein for the undoing of his toil. The tit is as industrious a worker in the garden as the starling, and, unlike the starling, he has no taste for my cherries. A pair of blue tits have been observed to carry a caterpillar to their nest on an average every two minutes for the greater part of the day. That is the sort of bird that deserves encouragement—a bird that loves caterpillars and does not love cherries. There are very few creatures with so clean a record. So hang out the coco-nut as a sign of goodwill.

And yet, as I write, I am reminded that in this imperfect world where no unmixed blessing is vouchsafed to us, even the tit does not escape the general law of qualified beneficence. For an hour past I have been agreeably aware of the proximity of a great tit who, from a hedge below the orchard, has been singing his little see-saw song with unremitting industry. Now behold him. There he goes flitting and pirouetting with that innocent grace which, as he skips in and out of the hedge just in front of you, suggests that he is inviting you to a game of hide-and-seek. But not now. Now he is revealing the evil that dwells in the best of us. Now he reminds us that he too is a part of that nature which feeds so relentlessly on itself. See him over the hives, glancing about in his own erratic way and taking his bearings. Then, certain that the coast is clear, he nips down and taps upon one of the hives with his beak. He skips away to await results. The trick succeeds; the doorkeeper of the hive comes out to inquire into the disturbance, and down swoops the great tit and away he flies with his capture. An artful fellow in spite of his air of innocence.

There is no affectation of innocence about that robust fellow the starling. He is almost as candid a ruffian as the rook, and three months hence I shall hate him with an intensity that would match Caligula's " Oh, that the Romans had only one neck! " For then he will come out of the beech woods on the hill-side for his great annual spring offensive against my cherry trees, and in two or three days he will leave them an obscene picture of devastation, every twig with its desecrated fruit and the stones left bleaching in the sun. But in these days of February I can be just even to my enemy. I can admit without reserve that he is not all bad any more than the other winsome little fellow is all good. See him on autumn or winter days when he has mobilized his forces for his forages in the fields, and his carrying out those wonderful evolutions in the sky that are such a miracle of order and rhythm. Far off, the cloud approaches like a swirl of dust in the sky, expanding, contracting, changing formation, breaking up into battalions, merging into columns, opening out on a wide front, throwing out flanks and advance guards and rear guards, every complication unravelled in perfect order, every movement as serene and assured as if the whole cloud moved to the beat of some invisible conductor below—a very symphony of the air, in which motion merges into music, until it seems that you are not watching a flight of birds, but listening with the inner ear to great waves of soundless harmony. And then, the overture over, down the cloud descends upon the fields, and the farmers' pests vanish before the invasion. And if you will follow them into the fields you will find infinite tiny holes that they have drilled and from which they have extracted the lurking enemy of the crops, and you will remember that it is to their beneficial activities that we owe the extermination of the May beetle, whose devastations were so menacing a generation ago. And after the flock has broken up and he has paired, and the responsibilities of housekeeping have begun, he continues his worthy labours. When spring has come you can see him dart from his nest in the hollow of the tree and make a journey a minute to the neighbouring field, returning each time with a chafer-grub or a wireworm or some other succulent but pestiferous morsel for the young and clamorous family at home. That acute observer Mr. G. G. Desmond says that he has counted eighteen such journeys in fifteen minutes. What matter a few cherries for a fellow of such benignant spirit?

But wait, my dear sir, wait until June brings the ripening cherries and see how much of this magnanimity of February is left.

Sir, I refuse to be intimidated by June or any other consideration. Sufficient unto the day——— And to-day I will think only good of the sturdy fellow in the coat of mail. To-day I will think only of the brave news that is abroad. It has got into the hives. On fine days such as this stray bees sail out for water, bringing the

agreeable tidings that all is well within, that the queen
bee is laying her eggs, "according to plan," and that
moisture is wanted in the hive. There are a score of
hives in the orchard, and they have all weathered the
winter and its perils. We saw the traces of one of those
perils when the snow still lay on the ground. Around
each hive were the footmarks of a mouse. He had come
from a neighbouring hedge, visited each hive in turn,
found there was no admission, and had returned to the
hedge no doubt hungrier than he came. Poor little
wretch! To be near such riches, lashings of sweetness
and great boulders of wax, and not be able to get bite
or sup. I see him trotting back through the snow to
his hole, a very dejected mouse. Oh, these new-fangled
hives that don't give a fellow a chance!

In the garden the news is coming up from below,
borne by those unfailing outriders of the spring, the
snowdrop and the winter aconite. A modest company;
but in their pennons is the assurance of the many-
coloured host that is falling unseen into the vast pageant
of summer and will fill the woods with the trumpets of
the harebell and the wild hyacinth, and make the
hedges burst into foam, and the orchard a glory of pink
and white, and the ditches heavy with the scent of the
meadowsweet, and the fields golden with harvest and
the gardens a riot of luxuriant life. I said it was all
right, chirps little red waistcoat from the fence—all the
winter I've told you that there was a good time coming
and now you see for yourself. Look at those flowers.
Ain't they real? The philosopher in the red waistcoat
is perfectly right. He has kept his end up all through
the winter, and has taken us into his fullest confidence.

Formerly he never came beyond the kitchen, but this winter when the snow was about he advanced to the parlour where he pottered about like one of the family. Now, however, with the great news outside and the earth full of good things to pick up, he has no time to call.

Even up in the woods that are still gaunt with winter and silent, save for the ringing strokes of the wood-cutters in some distant clearing, the message is borne in the wind that comes out of the west at the dawn of the spring, and is as unlike the wind of autumn as the spirit of the sunrise is unlike the spirit of the sunset. It is the lusty breath of life coming back to the dead earth, and making these February days the most thrilling of the year. For in these expanding skies and tremors of life and unsealings of the secret springs of nature all is promise and hope, and nothing is for regret and lament. It is when fulfilment comes that the joy of possession is touched with the shadow of parting. The cherry blossom comes like a wonder and goes like a dream, carrying the spring with it, and the dirge of summer itself is implicit in the scent of the lime trees and the failing note of the cuckoo. But in these days of birth when

Youth, inexpressibly fair, wakes like a wondering rose,

there is no hint of mortality and no reverted glance. The curtain is rising and the pageant is all before us.

" ALPHA OF THE PLOUGH "—*Windfalls.*

WINTER

To town and country Winter comes alike, but to each he comes in different fashion. To the villager, he stretches a bold, frosty hand; to the townsman, a clammy one. To the villager, he comes wrapt in cold clear air; to the townsman, in yellow fogs, through which the gas-lamps blear at noon. To the villager, he brings snow on the bare trees, frosty spangles on the roadways, exquisite silver chasings and adornments to the ivies on the walls, tumults of voices and noises of skating-irons, smouldering orange sunsets that disdain the snows, make brazen the window-panes, and fire even the icicles at the cottage eaves. To the townsman, he brings influenzas, secret slides on unlighted pavements, showers of snow-balls from irreverent urchins, damp feet, avalanches from the roofs of houses six stories high, cab fares woefully begrudged, universal slush. Winter is like a Red Indian, noble in his forests and solitudes, deteriorated by cities and civilization. The signs of his approach are different in the town and in the village. To a certain northern city, whose spires fret my sky-line of a morning, his proximity is made known by the departure of the last tourist and the arrival of the first student; by brown papers taken from windows in fashionable streets and squares; by the reassembling of schools and academies; and by advertisements in the newspapers relative to the opening of the University. By these signs, rather than by the cawing of uneasy rooks, or the whirling away of the last red leaf, the inhabitants know that the stern season is at hand; a salvo of inaugural addresses announces that he is in their midst, and the reappearance of lawyers in the long-deserted halls of the Parliament House, is regarded as a prophecy of snow. In that famous northern city, winter is disagreeable, as in other cities. Lawyers, doctors and professors tumble out of bed, and shave by gas-light. The entire population catches cold, and the clergymen are coughed down on Sundays. The falling snow covers the pavements—except the spaces in front of the bakers' shops, which are wet, and black, and steaming; in due time it makes dumb the streets, muffling every sound of wheel and hoof; it slips its moorings, and hangs in icicles and avalanches from the roofs of houses, but it does not appear in any perfection; it has lost all purity, and is dingy as a city sparrow. It is regarded as a nuisance; shopkeepers scrape it from their doors, deft scavengers build it in mounds along the streets; in a couple of days thaw sets in, and from roof, and eave, and cornice, from window-sill, gargoyle, and spout, there is a universal sound of weeping, like that which was heard in the old Norse world, when gods and men lamented the death of Balder the Beautiful. On frosty mornings, cab-horses, whose shoes are never sharpened in preparation, although the previous night every star was sparkling like steel, are tumbling on the hilly streets, and the fare gesticulates from the window, and one man holds down the head of the terrified animal, whose breath is like a wreath of incense, and the driver, clothed in a drab great-coat, with a comforter up to his nose, is busy with the girths, and small boys gather round, and attempt to blow some warmth into their benumbed fingers. Up from the sea comes a wicked *harr*, shedding disastrous twilight; church spires are visible half way up and disappear; the lights in shops are yellow smears on the darkness; at crossings, vehicles burst on you in a moment, and in another moment are swallowed up; and on the obscure pavement all ties of relationship and acquaintanceship are dissolved. Men are strangers for the time being; without a sinking of the heart, debtor brushes clothes with creditor; and with never a thrill Romeo steps off the pavement to let Juliet pass, quite unconscious that his divinity is near. Even on the more favourable days there is little to please one in a wintry city; overhead the smoke hangs heavily and lazily; for an hour or so a small uninteresting sun is stuck on the murky sky, like a red wafer on a dirty letter, and the setting is accomplished as rapidly as possible, and without any attempt at pomp. The south-west will not even turn out a corporal's guard to present arms to such a visitor. The townsman does not care for Winter, although he may care for what Winter brings—the long lighted evenings in which he can read or work, the lectures, the dinner-parties, the concerts, the theatres, and, if very young, the sprig of mistletoe stuck under the chandelier of a Christmas night.

But in this quiet place—distant but a few miles from the city of which I have been speaking—Winter is as pleasant as summer in her prime. To this village,

Winter sends other *avant couriers* than the taking down of brown paper from the windows of great houses, or the advertisement of college sessions. The rooks gathering in the coloured woods was one sign; the ploughing of the wheat-fields was another. The reddening of the beech hedges told me Winter was on his way. The Robin hopping along the shrubbery walks in his search for crumbs—remembering well they were scattered there last year—told me he was at hand. The rime of a morning on the old walls outside told me he was already come. One could feel the impalpable presence in the crisp air, in the clear blue distance with the castle and city spires etched upon it, in the stillness broken only by the rustle of a withered leaf, in the bright yet sobered sunlight, in the quickened current of the blood as one walked. Sated whilom with foliage, in my rambles my eye delights in naked branches, and I please myself with noting how many objects become visible at this season which summer had kept secret; ragged nests high up in trees, houses and farm buildings standing amongst woods, bridges and fences, and the devious courses of streams. These things are lost and buried in the leafiness of summer, and are only to be recognized now, as truths are discerned in age which youth never guesses of. When I return, the sunset is burning away behind the stripes of ancient pines that stand on the scarped bank above the stream, making their bronzed trunks yet more red—yet more dark their undecaying verdure. And by the last gleam on the distant hills, I notice that their crests are hoary. Snow, then, has already come, and will be with us anon.

Winter in the country, without snow, is like a summer

without the rose. Snow is Winter's specialty, its crown-
ing glory, its last exquisite grace. Snow comes naturally
in Winter, as foliage comes in summer; but although
one may have been familiar with it during forty seasons,
it always takes one with a certain pleased surprise and
sense of strangeness. In each Winter the falling of the
first snow-flake is an event; it lays hold of the imagination. A child does not ordinarily take notice of the
coming of leaves and flowers, but it will sit at a window
for an hour, watching the descent of the dazzling
apparition, with odd thoughts and fancies in the little
brain. Snow attracts the child as the plumage of some
rare and foreign bird would. The most prosaic of
mortals, when he comes downstairs of a morning, and
finds a new soft, white world, instead of the hard,
familiar black one, is conscious of some obscure feeling
of pleasure, the springs of which he might find it difficult
to explain. I do not care much for snow in town; but
in the country it is ever a marvel: it wipes out all bound-
ary lines and distinctions between fields; it clothes the
skeletons of trees with a pure wonder; through the
strangely transfigured landscape the streams run black
as ink and without a sound; and over all, the cold blue
frosty heaven smiles as if in very pleasure at its work.
On such a day, how windless and composed the atmosphere, how bright the frosty sunlight, from what a
distance comes a shout or the rusty caw of a rook!
" Earth hath not anything to show more fair." And
somehow the season seems to infuse a spirit of jollity
into everything. As I walk about I fancy the men I
meet look ruddier and healthier; that they talk in louder
and cheerier tones; that their chests heave with a

sincerer laughter. They are more charitable, I know. Winter binds " earth-born companions and fellow-mortals " together, from man to red-breast; and interior domestic life takes a new charm from the strange pallor outside. The good creature Fire feels exhilarated, and licks with its pliant tongue, as if pleased and flattered. Sofa and slippers become luxuries. The tea-urn purrs like a fondled cat. In those long, warm-lighted evenings, books communicate more of their inmost souls than they do in summer; and a moment's glance at the village church roof, sparkling to the frosty moon, adds warmth to fleecy blankets, and a depth to repose.

The white flakes are coming at last! Stretch out your hand—the meteor falls into it lighter than a rose-leaf, and is in a moment a tear. It is as fragile as beautiful. How innocent in appearance the new-fallen snow, the surface of which a descending leaf would dimple almost! and yet there is nothing fiercer, deadlier, crueller, more treacherous. On wild uplands and moors it covers roads and landmarks, and makes the wanderer travel hopeless miles till he sinks down exhausted; it steeps his senses in a pleasing stupor, till he fancies he sees the light of his far-off dwelling, and hears the voices of his children, who will be orphans before the morn; it smites him on the mouth and face as he dies, and then covers him up, softly as with kisses, tenderly as with eiderdown, like a sleek-white murderer as it is. In alliance with the demon of wind, it will drift and spin along the mountain-sides, and in a couple of hours a hundred sheep and their shepherd are smothered in a corry on Ben Nevis. Welded by frost into an avalanche, it slides from its dizzy hold, and falls on an Alpine village, crushing it to powder. A snowflake is weak in itself, but in multitudes it is omnipotent. These terrible crystals have stayed the marches of conquerors and broken the strength of empires. The innumerous flakes flying forth on the Russian wind are deadlier than bullets; they bite more bitterly than Cossack lances. In front, behind, on every side, for leagues and leagues they fall in the dim twilight, flinging themselves in front of the weary soldier's foot, clogging the wheels of cannon, making the banner an icy sheet, stilling the drum that beats the charge. O weary soldiers of the Empire, eyes that saw the sun of Austerlitz, hearts that love Napoleon—to this grim battle with Winter, Lodi and Arcola were holiday parades! The Loire will murmur from antique town to town, through pleasant summer lands of France, till it rests in the Spanish sea; vines stretched from pole to pole will glow in setting suns; girls will dance at village festivals; but for you, never more the murmuring river, nor the ripening grape, nor the dancing girl's waist and smile. For you the deadly snow-kisses, the sleep and the dreams that bring death, the dreadful embalming of frosts, potent as the spices that preserve Pharaoh.

At home, Winter is a terrible despot; but like the wild Goths which he nurtured, he becomes more civilized as he travels south. Like a travelled man of the world, he adapts himself to the countries in which he sojourns. The ice, which is misery at Labrador, is luxury at Naples. In our country we know Winter chiefly in his mild and fanciful moods. In England he is artist and adorner. He brightens the bloom on the cheeks of girls; he breathes the quaintest forests on our bedroom windows; he beards cottage eaves with icicles; he makes the lake

a floor on which the skater may disport himself; he fires
the south-west with sober sunsets; he gives star and
planet a metallic lustre. But with all these pleasant
qualities and obliging graces, he wears here, as at home,
the old heart. Have you not seen him in our own streets
pinch cruelly a poor child scantily clad? Do we not
know how he maltreats the desolate widow and the
unemployed artisan? Do we not hear of him in savage
mood killing outright poor homeless wretches whom
he has discovered asleep on stairs or in deserted cellars?
Here, as I have said, he is partially civilized, but at home
he is a despot; there he piles the iceberg that sails south-
ward to crush ships; there he pinches the starved wolf;
there he makes the Esquimaux shiver through all his
furs. And the Arctic voyagers whom he takes prisoner
and locks up in his immeasurable dungeons of snow and
ice, *they* know what a Giant Despair he is; and friends
at home who wait and wait, and to whom no news ever
comes, know it too.

There is one more good thing about Winter—he
brings Christmas. Through the bleak December the
thought of the coming festival is pleasant—like the
reflection of a fire on our faces. We taste the cake before
it is baked, and when it is actually before us we find
that it is none the worse for the fond handling of
imagination. Christmas Day is the pleasantest day in
the whole year. On that day we think tenderly of
distant friends; we strive to forgive injuries—to close
accounts with ourselves and the world—to begin the
new year with a white leaf, and a trust that the chapter
of life about to be written will contain more notable
entries, a fairer sprinkling of good actions, fewer erasures

made in blushes, and fewer ugly blots than some of the earlier ones. And to make Christmas perfect, the ground should be covered and the trees draped with snow; the bleak world outside should make us enjoy all the more keenly the comforts we possess; and, above all, it should make us remember the poor and the needy; for a charitable deed is the best close of any chapter of our lives, and the best promise, too, for the record about to be begun.

We are accustomed to consider Winter the grave of the year, but it is not so in reality. In the stripped trees, the mute birds, the disconsolate gardens, the frosty ground, there is only an apparent cessation of Nature's activities. Winter is a pause in music, but during the pause the musicians are privately tuning their strings, to prepare for the coming outburst. When the curtain falls on one piece at the theatre, the people are busy behind the scenes making arrangements for that which is to follow. Winter is such a pause, such a fall of the curtain. Underground, beneath snow and frost, next spring and summer are secretly getting ready. The roses which young ladies will gather six months hence for hair or bosom, are already in hand. In Nature there is no such thing as paralysis. Each thing flows into the the other, as movement into movement in graceful dances; Nature's colours blend in imperceptible gradation; all her notes are sequacious. I go out to my garden and notice that when the last leaves have fallen off my lilac and currant-bushes, like performers at the side-wings waiting their turn to come on, the new buds are all ready. To-day I beheld great knobs of buds on a horse-chestnut of mine, liquored over with an oily exudation which glittered in the sunlight. In my plants, the life which in June and July was exuberant in blossom and odour, has withdrawn to the root, where it lies *perdue*, taking counsel with itself regarding the course of action to be adopted next season. The spring of 1864 is even now underground, and the first snows will hardly have melted till it will peep out timorously in snowdrops; then, bolder grown, will burst in crocuses, holding up their coloured lamps; then, by fine grada-tions, the floral year will reach its noon, the rose; then, by fine gradations, it will die in a sunset of hollyhocks and tiger-lilies; and so we come again to withered leaves and falling snows.

ALEXANDER SMITH—*Last Leaves.*

LONDONERS

IT is the mark of a townsman to feed birds. No one in the country would think of feeding birds, except caged birds, or tits, or pigeons, or fowl, or during a frost. There is food, indeed, in every tree and in every garden and in every field. To throw breadcrumbs to birds in such circumstances would be merely a rather ridiculous hobby, like flinging pennies to be scrambled for by peers on their way to the House of Lords. In London conditions are changed. Here the birds are beggars and dependent on our charity. The black-headed gulls swoop down in procession by Blackfriars Bridge, each with a beggar's whine. The ducks in the parks stand on their heads for halfpence. The sparrows, if you have so much as a crust of bread on you, will gather round you like guttersnipes demanding " mouldies." Many people speak ill of sparrows. I can understand dislike of them in the country, but I cannot understand it in the town. In the country they are invaders, driving out of the neighbourhood better birds than themselves. Other birds apparently regard them as low, and will not consort in the same garden with them. They will not, at least, make friends, and they have a happier air when the sparrows are gone. In town, on the other hand, the sparrow is at home. He does not keep the other birds away, for they would not come in any case. He has no music for the traffic to drown—no bright plumage for the smoke to blacken. He is a little parasite, who can pick up a living where a more sensitive bird would starve. He is cheeky, Cockney, insuppressible. He is, in a sense, vicious. He will go through a bed of crocuses and break their necks with as little compunction as a fox destroying geese. It would not be so bad if he really wanted to eat the crocuses, but it is as though he actually enjoyed wasting them. He leaves them lying, yellow and purple and white, like a battle-field of flowers. No cat was ever more cruel. But, apart from this, I do not see what can be said against him by the townsman. How charming a little dancer he is as he hops in scores and in fifties round a Londoner who has bread—hops backwards and forwards like a marionette or like someone whose feet have been tied together for fun, or like a small child hopping up and down in sheer excitement. He may not, as an individual, be so confiding as the robin. But the robins do not come dancing round a human being in families like the family of the old woman who lived in a shoe. They are selfish birds, and no robin will share a human being with another robin. Sparrows are sociable, like a crowd of children begging from a tourist. They may be greedy; they may fight over the spoils; but their vices are the vices of creatures that love the company of their kind.

The seagull, however, seems to me to be a more interesting London bird than the sparrow. The seagull is a bird that can spy a piece of bread almost as far as a vulture can spy a corpse. It is impossible to enter one of the London parks with a piece of dry bread in your pocket without every seagull knowing it for a mile around. I was standing by the Round Pond the other day, when a small girl came up with a paper bag full of bread to feed the ducks. She opened the bag and, taking out a slice that had seen better days, said to me gravely, " Would *you* like a bit? " I felt it would be ungracious to refuse, and no sooner had she passed me the slice of bread than a cloud of gulls came falling down out of the sky, each gull with a different-sized brown patch on its head. They whirled about us with such clamour that there was nothing to be done but begin to feed them. I have never before thrown bread at seagulls, but I found it extraordinarily satisfying. It was like watching the most brilliant possible fielding at cricket.

It may be that in time one learns to distinguish between the cleverness of one bird and the cleverness of another in catching fragments of bread on the wing. Sometimes a catch is missed, and the bread has to be retrieved from among the ducks in the water. But as a rule one of the birds proves its genius by breaking out of the crowd and intercepting the bread at the beginning of its fall with open beak. There is certainly enough variety of catching and missing to prevent feeding the seagulls from ever becoming tedious. It would, I fancy, be rather monotonous if it were not for this constant element of doubt. Every time one throws bread into the air, however, one has a sort of gambler's interest in what is going to happen. One is playing with the unknown. The permutations and combinations of chance are as numerous, perhaps, in the

feeding of seagulls as in anything else. **To the out-**
sider it may seem a foolish and infantile hobby, but
it is clear that it must be a more prolific field of experi-
ence than the outsider realizes. I am only a beginner
at it, but it seems to me already as though I had discovered an occupation that will leave me little time for
anything else on Saturday and Sunday mornings. It
is one of the few amusements that seem always to come
to an end before one is tired. As you throw the last
corner of the last slice of bread you have brought into
the scramble of birds, you regret with a pang that you
did not bring twice as much. You feel that you had
only begun to enjoy yourself; besides, you feel that the
birds are still as hungry as ever, if in fact they have not
become even hungrier as a result of being fed. At least
that is what I imagine you feel. I felt it by proxy as I
watched the little girl searching for the ultimate crumb
in the two corners of her paper bag. This may only
have been the enthusiasm of an initiate: once I felt as
enthusiastic about philology, about postage stamps,
about hens. What child that has ever lived much on a
farm believes that the interest of hens can ever come to
an end? It is not merely that he can name the breed
of every hen in the yard—Spanish, Leghorn, Dorking,
Cochin China, Brahmaputra, Game, Bantam, Buff
Orpington, and all the rest—but he knows the life, the
habits and the appetites of each. He knows them as
mothers; he knows which of them lays the most charming eggs; he knows which of them is the greediest and
always arrives first with long, foolish strides beside the
scattered banquet of mash. He knows the very chickens
all but by name. He remembers the first effort of the

young Dorking cockerel to crow like his father—a noise
as though a gramophone gargled. He notices the un-
gainly, feathery legs of another overgrown cockerel, and,
being reminded of a figure in the Scriptures, names him
" Lazarus rising from the dead." He also knows every
loose-liver in the yard—immoral hens that do not lay
in the orthodox nests, but make nests of their own in the
plantation across the road, or under a haystack or in a
dark corner of the barn. Hens, indeed, are to him a
crowded world, as some tribe of savages who would bore
you and me are to an eager anthropologist. We may
take it as certain that there is this infinite variety in any
corner of life into which we peer with sufficient intensity
of vision. The man of science looking through a microscope at a drop of water sees a world of living creatures
of which the rest of us know nothing but by hearsay.
If his microscrope were strong enough, no doubt he
would learn to distinguish each of these infinitesimal
creatures from each other, and give each of them a
separate name, as a farmer gives separate names to his
cows. If his microscope were stronger still, he might
discover within one of these infinitesimal creatures an
apparently infinite number of still tinier living creatures,
and so on, worlds without end.

Hence it seems reasonable to suppose that the study
of seagulls alone might keep a man interested and still
making new discoveries for a lifetime. At present I
know nothing about them, except that they have an
endless appetite for bread that even a restaurant
proprietor would shrink from putting into a cabinet
pudding. But I know enough to make me understand
and envy the people who stand on the Embankment

and on the bridges and bring a world of white birds down about their heads to share their poor luncheons. Some people love throwing things to a dog—biscuits, lumps of sugar, etc.—but to feed the seagulls is as good as throwing things to a wilderness of dogs.

Then there are ducks. The countryman may boast of his nightingales, his larks, his woodpeckers, his king-fishers, his jays. But, after all, the ducks on the Serpentine have points of superiority to any of these birds. They, too, will repay you if you take your courage in both hands and go out boldly with bread in a paper bag. How nobly they ride the ripples of the stormy pond, awaiting the bread-giver! How, on catching a distant sight of him, they hasten like a fleet of small motor boats to his neighbourhood! How exquisitely the blue feather shines out of the drab in the wing even of the dullest duck! How gorgeously the drake's head gleams with shifting blue and green lights! How lordlily his tail curls! Was ever pig's tail prettier? Then there are the tufted ducks, each with its straight back hair blowing about in the wind like the straight back hair of a quack dentist, or a piano-tuner, or an elocution master. Each of them, too, has a little round eye as yellow as bright sunshine, and each of them has the gift of standing on its head and performing feats as dexterous as the cart-wheels of a street arab. I saw a small ragged boy in Hyde Park last week amusing a baby in a perambulator extemporized out of a sugar-box by throwing small stones among the tufted ducks. I dislike the habit of throwing stones at ducks, and, though none of them seemed to be hitting the birds, I felt nervous for their little daffodil eyes. I spoke my mind about it—not to the small boy, for I am always afraid that if I reprove people my pulpit blood may assert itself—but in an aside to a lady. She went across to him, and instead of treating him as a brand to be plucked from the burning, as I should have done, she spoke to him almost as a fellow-sinner. "You're taking care not to hit any of them, aren't you?" she said, smiling. He turned up an enthusiastic face on which there was a large smudge on each cheek and a large smudge on his small nose. He was just big enough to be able to walk and talk without accident. He beamed good nature and said in a series of gasps of excitement: "You throws things at 'em, and they stands on their 'eads." It was certainly true. The tufted ducks were standing on their heads, peering after the sunk pebbles in the hope that they were bread, till they must have been giddy. As I watched them my attitude to the youngster changed. I, too, had rather see a duck standing on its head than almost any other sort of acrobat. I love to see the uneasy equilibrium, and the kicking legs with the joints going up and down like piston-rods. Besides, it amused the baby. Was it virtuous? I do not know. If one of the ducks had been hit, my attitude would probably have changed back again to the normal, and I should have spoken my mind angrily—to the lady. But no harm was done beyond giving the ducks headaches. . . .

But the subject of ducks is endless. Have you ever seen a teal? Why, a teal alone is the beginning of a story as long as *The Arabian Nights*.

ROBERT LYND—*Solomon in All His Glory*.

THE HOP LEAF

" WHICH would have enchanted me as a boy "—the
words linger. I can fairly say, not forgetting those
miseries which childhood only understands as miseries,
that life was not so bad in that Kentish village before
the war.   London was within forty miles of us, but
troubled most of the inhabitants hardly more than the
mountains of the moon.   The county town was the real
metropolis, and after all it was quite a business to get
there on the market train of a Saturday afternoon.
That train, I recall, was the famous 2.23 : but if it came
huffily into our station before three o'clock we counted
ourselves lucky.   And, after all, why make haste?
The river beside the line seldom did so, mirroring his
magnificent old willows in deep tranquillity.   The crows
flapped lazily over the molehilly pastures, where the
boy who minded the cow had gone to sleep below the
chestnut-trees.

  Slow?   You might accuse us of being so, but we
should have been puzzled and obstinate.   Excitement
is to be measured by individual standard, and the
circling year brought enough for the desires of that
microcosm on the somnolent Medway.   A thing was
none the worse there for being old.   Curious as it may

appear in a few years' time, the village church was the centre and source of many notable events. Folks were proud of that church, in the pews of which were prayer books that had not been moved many yards since the spacious days of George the Third, in the tower of which were six bells commemorating ancient churchwardens still represented in the parish by their posterity. It was a sizable church, but the evening service often filled it, and harvest thanksgiving packed the aisles as well as the pews with pleased labourers and tradesmen.

Perhaps the greatest chapter in those calmly unfolding volumes of kindly time was that headed " The New Organ." In those days the organist was an unusually choice musician, and his complaints against the old and capricious instrument, followed by his energetic collection towards a new one, brought success. The public often looked in with agreeable cold thrills as the workmen turned up bones and even skulls from the church floor. Every one told every one else that the new organ's bellows were to be blown by " hyadraulic pressure "; such expressions as " detached console " and " combination stops " (always affably explained by the gifted organist) were to be heard in the parlour of the " George " Inn. When at last the miraculous new organ was ready for opening, a gorgeous ceremony was held; quite a staff of clergymen shared the service, one of whom preached on " Church Music " with such eloquence that the choir-boys stopped eating black currant lozenges; the organist himself struck out inimitable chords at those passages of the psalms which referred to thunder, lightning, dragons and so on, and a still more agile performer from a college chapel supplemented such glories with a recital that seemed to make the purple of the painted windows turn pale.

Other high days which Mother Church gave us could readily be recounted; even funerals used to be considered one of life's advantages (more or less); but recollection hurries on to secular blessings. That village had a cricket ground almost as smooth and level as a billiard table, and two teams supported our reputation, the first consisting of the aristocrats, as farmers, brewers, doctors, the clergy, and " visitors "; the second enlisting such humbler sportsmen, as the village schoolmaster, butcher, farm bailiffs, railway clerks, footmen, and simple Hodge. The excitement of all matches in which these teams (but particularly the second) took part almost takes my breath away even at this time. The chorus which used to reverberate through the lanes as they drove home in white-blossomed twilight from far-away matches had a genuine jollity worthy of Mr. Pickwick's notebook.

In winter came football, but its sovereignty was as yet far from being acknowledged. Old men were wont to become offensively jocular when they heard that one had been watching or playing this game. Only a few spectators, cheered with local ales and stouts, watched our wandering boys " roosh and tear and hollar-blare " through the November mud; these few supporters had not the modern football crowd's vocabulary, and monthly alternated " Let's 'Ave Another We Go " with " Set 'Em Alight " or " Tie A Bit of Cotton On It." This last phrase referred to monstrous soaring kicks, in which the barrel-shaped butcher's roundman excelled.

This particular village rejoices in its water-courses; there is the Medway, parent stream; there are also two or three little confluents which Spenser in his *Faerie Queene* and Drayton in his *Polyolbion* have not grudged to honour in Elizabethan metaphor. Only the curate and the village schoolmaster knew of that, but nobody would have been surprised to hear it. These waters were good for fishing, and all of us went a-fishing; indeed, persons from London and even the industrial north arrived with all their gaudy tackle and (it was felt) somewhat too assertive manners, to tempt our shoals. The first day of the season was always pounced upon like a crock of gold; few came home at that jubilant beginning without a stick full of nice fish; but afterward the survivors in the pools knew a thing or two about incomplete and complete anglers. It was in those monotonous periods that some of the elder men would outwear the patience of the heavy grey bream and strong-backed chub, or the savage energy of some noted pike; and, returning through the dewy darkness, would be seen showing the catch to a friend, and provide a nine days' wonder.

As summer grew middle-aged and a little grey, the season of hop-picking arrived with unfailing activity and excitement, in the local sense of the word. Our meadows and copses, even some of the sacred lairs of our redoubtable anglers, were then invaded by the annual tribes from the East End or the slums of Brighton; no place was too venerable for these joyful and blasphemous marauders. However, the actual business of hop-picking, which occupies almost all of daylight, kept them from taking us, and our damsons, entirely by storm. They came in families, and alliances of families, to " take on " as last year with the farmer whose mien and pay pleased best. It must be a wonderful holiday, hop-picking, for those who ordinarily have to fight for a little sun and air in mean streets, and there used to be many a smile as the measurer and the bookkeeper moved among the bins of those hop-pickers. " 'Ere, there's ahr little bookie. Hi, Bookie." " I remember you, sir, that I do—lawst year I 'ad to stay 'ome, but I remember you " —such cries of recognition cheered the opening day of hop-picking. The same old fellows as ever in football jerseys and patchwork trousers appeared opposite the village stores to do a roaring trade in dried fish, clothing, gaudy sweets, bottled mysteries; the same brawls took place outside the " Two Brewers "—" She called our 'op-'ouse a stinkin' monkey-'ouse." " An' you 'it young Ike " (produced, holding hand to jaw), " on the chops, yer coward." Besides these personal differences, occasionally the pickers at some of the farms would strike, but how gently! A few hours, and all was proceeding as before, nor would any graver disturbance usually interrupt the ingathering of the hops, until at length the special train with cushionless seats carried back the Londoners to their homes, singing:

> " 'Oppin' is all over,
>   Money is all spent,
>   Don't I wish I'd never
>   Come 'oppin' dahn in Kent—
> Wiv a tee-ay-ay, tee-ay-ay, tee-ay-ee-ay-O! "

These were not our only visitors. At regular seasons the circus folk arrived, and the puffing engines which pulled their great wagons along scarcely puffed more than the small boys and girls who darted to the line

F*

of march.   The usual process of roundabouts, swing-boats, coco-nut shies, sword-swallowers and " try your strength " apparatus soon brought unearthly bliss to our midst, except where parents were too " respectable " or disciplinary.   I, for instance, was invariably forbidden to possess, carry, or use a water-pistol, and have been sharply criticized for entering the tent of " Howitzer George.   Has Won Upward of Sixty Belts in the West Country."   And one of our lads, always despised for ponderous inability in cricket, dared step into the ring (often looking out of it to his comrades, whose confidence was wonderful).   Well might we all join mightily in the psalm the following Sunday night, " The mountains skipped like rams."

Such soothing remembrances one owes to the rural community in the days of Edward the Seventh; I am writing about them as if they were ancient history, and to me they are.   It is years since I saw a man riding a tricycle, or that bicycle which has one wheel of Homeric dimension and the other like a quoit ring.   I do not know if the song-paper man still comes round with his long yellow broadsheets, and if he does they no more thrill our sweethearts and wives with the actual words of, " It's Only a Beautiful Picture," " As Soon as I Looked at my Seaweed," " It's not the Cage I'm After, It's the Bird," " And His Day's Work was Done." There is still hop-picking, but diminished, subdued—and mainly threatened.   Many kilns will never dry a poke-ful again.

The general dealer has his eye on " antiques "—bless us, what self-consciousness!   A soap factory has arisen by the station.   Our old home was sold recently as

" This Most Desirable Residence," and " within easy
reach of London."   But somehow the two fourteenth-
century bridges in the villages, of which I have a photo-
graph here, look just as far from London as when King
Edward was crowned, and in our celebrations our own
sailor home on leave climbed along the greasy pole fixed
from a parapet of one of them above the awesome pool,
and easily returned with the historic leg of mutton which
had baffled all other ambitions.

EDMUND BLUNDEN—*The Face of England.*

MACKERY END, IN HERTFORDSHIRE

BRIDGET ELIA has been my housekeeper for many a long year. I have obligations to Bridget, extending beyond the period of memory. We house together, old bachelor and maid, in a sort of double singleness; with such tolerable comfort, upon the whole, that I, for one, find in myself no sort of disposition to go out upon the mountains, with the rash king's offspring, to bewail my celibacy. We agree pretty well in our tastes and habits—yet so, as " with a difference." We are generally in harmony, with occasional bickerings—as it should be among near relations. Our sympathies are rather understood, than expressed; and once, upon my dissembling a tone in my voice more kind than ordinary, my cousin burst into tears, and complained that I was altered. We are both great readers in different directions. While I am hanging over (for the thousandth time) some passage in old Burton, or one of his strange contemporaries, she is abstracted in some modern tale, or adventure, whereof our common reading-table is daily fed with assiduously fresh supplies. Narrative teases me. I have little concern in the progress of events. She must have a story—well, ill, or indifferently told—so there be life stirring in it, and plenty of good or evil accidents. The fluctuations of fortune in fiction—and almost in real life—have ceased to interest, or operate but dully upon me. Out-of-the-way humours and opinions—heads with some diverting twist in them—the oddities of authorship, please me most. My cousin has a native disrelish of anything that sounds odd or bizarre. Nothing goes down with her, that is quaint, irregular, or out of the road of common sympathy. She "holds Nature more clever." I can pardon her blindness to the beautiful obliquities of the Religio Medici; but she must apologize to me for certain disrespectful insinuations, which she has been pleased to throw out latterly, touching the intellectuals of a dear favourite of mine, of the last century but one—the thrice noble, chaste and virtuous—but again somewhat fantastical, and original-brain'd, generous Margaret Newcastle.

It has been the lot of my cousin, oftener perhaps than I could have wished, to have had for her associates and mine, free-thinkers—leaders, and disciples, of novel philosophies and systems; but she neither wrangles with, nor accepts, their opinions. That which was good and venerable to her, when a child, retains its authority over her mind still. She never juggles or plays tricks with her understanding.

We are both of us inclined to be a little too positive; and I have observed the result of our disputes to be almost uniformly this—that in matters of fact, dates and circumstances, it turns out, that I was in the right, and my cousin in the wrong. But where we have differed upon moral points; upon something proper to be done, or let alone; whatever heat of opposition, or steadiness of conviction, I set out with, I am sure always, in the long run, to be brought over to her way of thinking.

I must touch upon the foibles of my kinswoman with a gentle hand, for Bridget does not like to be told of her faults. She hath an awkward trick (to say no worse of it) of reading in company: at which times she will answer *yes* or *no* to a question without fully understanding its purport—which is provoking, and derogatory in the highest degree to the dignity of the putter of the said question. Her presence of mind is equal to the most pressing trials of life, but will sometimes desert her upon trifling occasions. When the purpose requires it, and is a thing of moment, she can speak to it greatly; but in matters which are not stuff of the conscience, she hath been known sometimes to let slip a word less seasonably.

Her education in youth was not much attended to; and she happily missed all that train of female garniture, which passeth by the name of accomplishments. She was tumbled early, by accident or design, into a spacious closet of good old English reading, without much selection or prohibition, and browsed at will upon that fair and wholesome pasturage. Had I twenty girls, they should be brought up exactly in this fashion. I know not whether their chance in wedlock might not be diminished by it; but I can answer for it, that it makes (if the worst come to the worst) most incomparable old maids.

In a season of distress, she is the truest comforter; but in the teasing accidents, and minor perplexities, which do call out the *will* to meet them, she sometimes maketh matters worse by an excess of participation. If she does not always divide your trouble upon the pleasanter occasions of life she is sure always to treble your satisfaction. She is excellent to be at a play with, or upon a visit; but best when she goes a journey with you.

We made an excursion together a few summers since, into Hertfordshire, to beat up the quarters of some of our less-known relations in that fine corn country.

The oldest thing I remember is Mackery End; or Mackarel End, as it is spelt, perhaps more properly, in some old maps of Hertfordshire; a farm-house—delightfully situated within a gentle walk from Wheathampstead. I can just remember having been there, on a visit to a great-aunt, when I was a child, under the care of Bridget; who, as I have said, is older than myself by some ten years. I wish that I could throw into a heap the remainder of our joint existences, that we might share them in equal division. But that is impossible. The house was at that time in the occupation of a substantial yeoman, who had married my grandmother's sister. His name was Gladman. My grandmother was a Bruton, married to a Field. The Gladmans and the Brutons are still flourishing in that part of the county, but the Fields are almost extinct. More than forty years had elapsed since the visit I speak of; and for the greater portion of that period, we had lost sight of the other two branches also. Who or what sort of persons inherited Mackery End—kindred or strange folk—we were afraid almost to conjecture, but determined some day to explore.

By somewhat a circuitous route, taking the noble park at Luton in our way from St. Albans, we arrived at the spot of our anxious curiosity about noon. The sight of the old farm-house, though every trace of it was effaced from my recollections, affected me with a pleasure which

I had not experienced for many a year. For though *I* had forgotten it, *we* had never forgotten being there together, and we had been talking about Mackery End all our lives, till memory on my part became mocked with a phantom of itself, and I thought I knew the aspect of a place, which, when present, O how unlike it was to *that*, which I had conjured up so many times instead of it!

Still the air breathed balmily about it; the season was in the " heart of June," and I could say with the poet,

> But thou, that didst appear so fair
>   To fond imagination,
> Dost rival in the light of day
>   Her delicate creation!

Bridget's was more a waking bliss than mine, for she easily remembered her old acquaintance again—some altered features, of course, a little grudged at. At first, indeed, she was ready to disbelieve for joy; but the scene soon reconfirmed itself in her affections—and she traversed every out-post of the old mansion, to the wood-house, the orchard, the place where the pigeon-house had stood (house and birds were alike flown) with a breathless impatience of recognition, which was more pardonable perhaps than decorous at the age of fifty-odd. But Bridget in some things is behind her years.

The only thing left was to get into the house—and that was a difficulty which to me singly would have been insurmountable; for I am terribly shy in making myself known to strangers and out-of-date kinsfolk. Love, stronger than scruple, winged my cousin in without me; but she soon returned with a creature that might have sat to a sculptor for the image of Welcome. It was the youngest of the Gladmans; who, by marriage with a Bruton, had become mistress of the old mansion. A comely brood are the Brutons. Six of them, females, were noted as the handsomest young women in the county. But this adopted Bruton, in my mind, was better than they all—more comely. She was born too late to have remembered me. She just recollected in early life to have had their cousin Bridget once pointed out to her, climbing a stile. But the name of kindred, and of cousinship, was enough. Those slender ties, that prove slight as gossamer in the rending atmosphere of a metropolis, bind faster, as we found it, in hearty, homely, loving Hertfordshire. In five minutes we were as thoroughly acquainted as if we had been born and bred up together; were familiar, even to the calling each other by our Christian names. So Christians should call one another. To have seen Bridget, and her—it was like the meeting of the two scriptural cousins! There was a grace and dignity, an amplitude of form and stature, answering to her mind, in this farmer's wife, which would have shined in a palace—or so we thought it. We were made welcome by husband and wife equally—we, and our friend that was with us.—I had almost forgotten him—but B.F.[1] will not so soon forget that meeting, if peradventure he shall read this on the far distant shores where the kangaroo haunts. The fatted calf was made ready, or rather was already so, as if in anticipation of our coming; and, after an appropriate glass of native wine, never let me forget with what honest pride this hospitable cousin made us proceed to

[1] Barron Field.

Wheathampstead, to introduce us (as some new-found rarity) to her mother and sister Gladmans, who did indeed know something more of us, at a time when she almost knew nothing.—With what corresponding kindness we were received by them also—how Bridget's memory, exalted by the occasion, warmed into a thousand half-obliterated recollections of things and persons, to my utter astonishment, and her own—and to the astoundment of B.F. who sat by, almost the only thing that was not a cousin there—old effaced images of more than half-forgotten names and circumstances still crowding back upon her, as words written in lemon come out upon exposure to a friendly warmth—when I forget all this, then may my country cousins forget me; and Bridget no more remember, that in the days of weakling infancy I was her tender charge—as I have been her care in foolish manhood since—in those pretty pastoral walks, long ago, about Mackery End, in Hertfordshire.

CHARLES LAMB—*The Essays of Elia.*

DREAMTHORP

I⊤ matters not to relate how or when I became a denizen of Dreamthorp; it will be sufficient to say that I am not a born native, but that I came to reside in it a good while ago now. The several towns and villages in which, in my time, I have pitched a tent did not please, for one obscure reason or another: this one was too large, t' other too small; but when, on a summer evening about the hour of eight, I first beheld Dreamthorp, with its westward-looking windows painted by sunset, its children playing in the single straggling street, the mothers knitting at the open doors, the fathers standing about in long white blouses, chatting or smoking; the great tower of the ruined castle rising high into the rosy air, with a whole troop of swallows—by distance made as small as gnats—skimming about its rents and fissures;— when I first beheld all this, I felt instinctively that my knapsack might be taken off my shoulders, that my tired feet might wander no more, that at last, on the planet, I had found a home. From that evening I have dwelt here, and the only journey I am like now to make, is the very inconsiderable one, so far at least as distance is concerned, from the house in which I live to the grave-yard beside the ruined castle. There, with the former

179

inhabitants of the place, I trust to sleep quietly enough, and nature will draw over our heads her coverlet of green sod, and tenderly tuck us in, as a mother her sleeping ones, so that no sound from the world shall ever reach us, and no sorrow trouble us any more.

The village stands far inland; and the streams that trot through the soft green valleys all about have as little knowledge of the sea, as the three-years' child of the storms and passions of manhood. The surrounding country is smooth and green, full of undulations; and pleasant country roads strike through it in every direction, bound for distant towns and villages, yet in no hurry to reach them. On these roads the lark in summer is continually heard; nests are plentiful in the hedges and dry ditches; and on the grassy banks, and at the feet of the bowed dikes, the blue-eyed speedwell smiles its benison on the passing wayfarer. On these roads you may walk for a year and encounter nothing more remarkable than the country cart, troops of tawny children from the woods, laden with primroses, and at long intervals—for people in this district live to a ripe age—a black funeral creeping in from some remote hamlet; and to this last the people reverently doff their hats and stand aside. Death does not walk about here often, but when he does, he receives as much respect as the squire himself. Everything round one is unhurried, quiet, moss-grown and orderly. Season follows in the track of season, and one year can hardly be distinguished from another. Time should be measured here by the silent dial, rather than by the ticking clock, or by the chimes of the church. Dreamthorp can boast of a respectable antiquity, and in it the trade of the builder is unknown. Ever since I remember, not a single stone has been laid on the top of another. The castle, inhabited now by jackdaws and starlings, is old; the chapel which adjoins it is older still; and the lake behind both, and in which their shadows sleep, is, I suppose, as old as Adam. A fountain in the market-place, all mouths and faces and curious arabesques—as dry, however, as the castle moat—has a tradition connected with it; and a great noble riding through the street one day several hundred years ago, was shot from a window by a man whom he had injured. The death of this noble is the chief link which connects the place with authentic history. The houses are old, and remote dates may yet be deciphered on the stones above the doors; the apple-trees are mossed and ancient; countless generations of sparrows have bred in the thatched roofs, and thereon have chirped out their lives. In every room of the place men have been born, men have died. On Dreamthorp centuries have fallen, and have left no more trace than have last winter's snowflakes. This commonplace sequence and flowing on of life is immeasurably affecting. That winter morning when Charles lost his head in front of the banqueting-hall of his own palace, the icicles hung from the eaves of the houses here, and the clown kicked the snowballs from his clouted shoon, and thought but of his supper when, at three o'clock, the red sun set in the purple mist. On that Sunday in June while Waterloo was going on, the gossips, after morning service, stood on the country roads discussing agricultural prospects, without the slightest suspicion that the day passing over their heads would be a famous one in the calendar. Battles have been fought, kings have died, history has transacted itself; but, all unheeding and untouched, Dreamthorp has watched apple-trees redden, and wheat ripen, and smoked its pipe, and quaffed its mug of beer, and rejoiced over its new-born children, and with proper solemnity carried its dead to the churchyard. As I gaze on the village of my adoption, I think of many things very far removed, and seem to get closer to them. The last setting sun that Shakespeare saw reddened the windows here, and struck warmly on the faces of the hinds coming home from the fields. The mighty storm that raged while Cromwell lay a-dying made all the oak-woods groan round about here, and tore the thatch from the very roofs I gaze upon. When I think of this, I can almost, so to speak, lay my hand on Shakespeare and on Cromwell. These poor walls were contemporaries of both, and I find something affecting in the thought. The mere soil is, of course, far older than either, but *it* does not touch one in the same way. A wall is the creation of a human hand, the soil is not.

This place suits my whim, and I like it better year after year. As with everything else, since I began to love it I find it gradually growing beautiful. Dreamthorp—a castle, a chapel, a lake, a straggling strip of grey houses, with a blue film of smoke over all—lies embosomed in emerald. Summer, with its daisies, runs up to every cottage door. From the little height where I am now sitting, I see it beneath me. Nothing could be more peaceful. The wind and the birds fly over it. A passing sunbeam makes brilliant a white gable-end, and brings out the colours of the blossomed apple-tree beyond, and disappears. I see figures in the street, but hear them not.

The hands on the church clock seem always pointing to one hour. Time has fallen asleep in the afternoon sunshine. I make a frame of my fingers, and look at my picture. On the walls of the next Academy's Exhibition will hang nothing half so beautiful!

My village is, I think, a special favourite of summer's. Every window-sill in it she touches with colour and fragrance; everywhere she wakens the drowsy murmurs of the hives; every place she scents with apple-blossom. Traces of her hand are to be seen on the weir beside the ruined mill; and even the canal, along which the barges come and go, has a great white water-lily asleep on its olive-coloured face. Never was velvet on a monarch's robe so gorgeous as the green mosses that be-ruff the roofs of farm and cottage, when the sunbeam slants on them and goes. The old road out towards the common, and the hoary dikes that might have been built in the reign of Alfred, have not been forgotten by the generous adorning season; for every fissure has its mossy cushion, and the old blocks themselves are washed by the loveliest grey-green lichens in the world, and the large loose stones lying on the ground have gathered to themselves the peacefulest mossy coverings. Some of these have not been disturbed for a century. Summer has adorned my village as gaily, and taken as much pleasure in the task, as the people of old, when Elizabeth was queen, took in the adornment of the May-pole against a summer festival. And, just think, not only Dreamthorp, but every English village she has made beautiful after one fashion or another—making vivid green the hill slope on which straggling white Welsh hamlets hang right opposite the sea; drowning in apple-blossom the red

Sussex ones in the fat valley. And think, once more, every spear of grass in England she has touched with a livelier green; the crest of every bird she has burnished; every old wall between the four seas has received her mossy and licheny attentions; every nook in every forest she has sown with pale flowers, every marsh she has dashed with the fires of the marigold. And in the wonderful night the moon knows, she hangs—the planet on which so many millions of us fight, and sin, and agonize, and die—a sphere of glow-worm light.

ALEXANDER SMITH—*Dreamthorp*. [Abridged]

NOTES

Joseph Addison and his friend Sir Richard Steele are best known for their creation, Sir Roger de Coverley, the lovable Tory Squire whom they introduced to English literature in the pages of *The Spectator*. Sir Roger has his country seat in Worcestershire and his town house in Soho Square. He is a member of the Spectator Club, and among his fellow members are Sir Andrew Freeport, Captain Sentry, Will Honeycomb and Mr. Spectator, the writer of the essays. In addition to the de Coverley essays Addison and Steele wrote on various aspects of contemporary life and manners. *The Adventures of a Shilling* appeared in another periodical called *The Tatler*.

" Alpha of the Plough " is the pen-name of Alfred G. Gardiner, journalist, essayist and editor. He was born at Chelmsford in 1865. For a number of years he was editor of the *Daily News*. In the volume of essays entitled *Pebbles on the Shore* the first essay tells how he came to choose his pen-name: "' As for your name, I offer you the whole firmament to choose from.' In that prodigal spirit the editor of the *Star* invites me to join. . . . And then my eye roves westward to where the Great Bear hangs head downwards as if to devour the earth. Great Bear, Charles's Wain, the Plough, the Dipper, the Chariot of David—with what fancies the human mind through all the ages has played with that glorious constellation! Let my fancy play with it too. There at the head of the Plough flames the great star that points to the pole. I will hitch my little wagon to that sublime image. I will be ' Alpha of the Plough.' "

BARBELLION is the pseudonym of Bruce Frederick Cummings, the author of two striking books: *The Journal of a Disappointed Man* and *Enjoying Life* from which the essay here reprinted has been taken. Born in 1889, he began his literary career while still a boy by contributing articles to *The Countryside*. Collecting birds' eggs, rearing pigeons and rabbits, constructing an ant's nest, watching and recording the ways of the wild creatures of the countryside were all part of his passionate interest in nature which filled his leisure hours when school work was done. His interest in living things went with a keen appreciation of good books from which he discovered he could observe life at second hand. While his small collection of books grew steadily, his specimens for observation soon began to find their way into the attic, and even into the kitchen! Unhappily his boyhood promise and his strong will were not matched with good fortune and strength of body, for when, without help, he had fought his way to a responsible post in the British Museum, his health suffered, and his feelings gave vent to that wonderful human document *The Journal of a Disappointed Man.*

EDMUND BLUNDEN was educated at Christ's Hospital and Queen's College, Oxford. During the war he served with the Royal Sussex Regiment. From 1924 to 1927 he was Professor of English Literature at Tokio University, and he is now Fellow and Tutor at Merton College, Oxford. The first collected edition of his poems was published in 1930 and in the same year he published a biography of Leigh Hunt.

DR. JOHN BROWN was born at Biggar, Lanarkshire. He studied medicine at Edinburgh University, and after a year as an assistant surgeon at Chatham returned to Edinburgh, took his degree of M.D., and began to practise as a physician. His leisure time he devoted to literature and his writings, which were contributed to various periodicals, were collected together under the title *Horæ Subsecivæ* ("Leisure Hours"). It is by his short tales and sketches such as *Rab and His Friends, Our Dogs* and *Jeems the Doorkeeper* that he is best known.

SIR JAMES GEORGE FRAZER, O.M., F.R.S., F.B.A., born at Glasgow in 1854, is our foremost authority on anthropology and folk-lore on which he has written numerous books. His "lighter" writings include the Greek legend *The Gorgon's Head* and the *Sir Roger de Coverley Essays*. Of the latter he writes, "Though I have borrowed the characters created by the genius of Addison, I have allowed them to act and talk after their own fashion, or what has appeared to me such, in scenes and circumstances conjured up by my own fancy and not by that of their illustrious creator."

OLIVER GOLDSMITH was poet, novelist, dramatist and essayist. He was born in Ireland, the son of a clergyman, and educated at Trinity College, Dublin. Then he proceeded to Edinburgh University as a student of medicine, but after eighteen months he tired of this study and set out on a tour of the Continent "with a guinea in his pocket, one shirt to his back and a flute in his hand." Returning to London he tried various professions, usher, printer's reader, apothecary's assistant, and finally he turned to writing for a living. His first poem *The Traveller* deals with his wanderings in Europe, but it is by *The Deserted Village* that he is perhaps best known as a poet. His novel is the *Vicar of Wakefield* and his best comedy *She Stoops to Conquer*. The most famous of his essays is the series known as *The Citizen of the World* or *Letters from a Chinese Philosopher residing in London to his Friends in the East*. In the guise of this Chinaman Goldsmith satirized English society and manners shrewdly and humorously just as

Addison had done in the rôle of Mr. Spectator. To Addison we owe Sir Roger de Coverley; to Goldsmith we owe Beau Tibbs, an equally delightful creation.

WILLIAM HENRY HUDSON, who was born on the South American pampas, has given us a delightful account of his happy boyhood in *Far Away and Long Ago*. When he was a boy of sixteen, however, he had a severe illness, and thereafter his life was a long struggle with ill-health and poverty. He came to England in 1869 and became a naturalized British subject in 1900. From his youngest days he was an intense observer of Nature, and especially of birds. "He was," said Galsworthy, "a distinguished naturalist, probably the most acute, broadminded and understanding of all observers of Nature." Among his books are: *Far Away and Long Ago, Afoot in England, The Book of a Naturalist, Nature in Downland, Hampshire Days*.

JAMES HENRY LEIGH HUNT was born at Southgate in Middlesex, and like Lamb and Coleridge was educated at Christ's Hospital. He became a journalist, and with his brother founded *The Examiner* and later *The Indicator*. A radical in politics he was imprisoned for two years for libelling the Prince Regent. During his imprisonment he was visited by such friends as Byron, Moore and Charles Lamb. His ambition was to succeed as a poet, but only one of his poems finds a place in anthologies, namely *Abou Ben Adhem*. It was as an essayist and literary critic that he was most successful.

WASHINGTON IRVING was the first American writer to gain a European reputation. Born in New York, the son of an Englishman, he studied for the legal profession, but as his health was delicate he travelled much both in America and

Europe. For a time he was in the diplomatic service of his country in England and Spain. His best known work is *The Sketch Book of Geoffrey Crayon, Gent,* a collection of short tales and sketches including *Rip Van Winkle* and *The Legend of Sleepy Hollow.*

FREDERIC WOOD JONES, F.R.S., born in London in 1879, is the learned Professor of Anatomy in the University of Melbourne. In the preface to *Unscientific Essays* he says, " These pages are the products of idle moments. Though a man's calling may be a well-defined one, and circum-scribed by narrow and traditional boundaries, it may yet be permitted to him to wander at times far away from his own small sphere. A blacksmith may meditate upon buttercups whilst he is shaving of a morning." He has continued to express the pleasures of his idle moments in *Unscientific Excursions.*

CHARLES LAMB was born in London and educated at Christ's Hospital where he had the poet Coleridge as a fellow-pupil. Prevented from entering the learned profes-sions by an impediment in his speech, he became a clerk in the South Sea House, and afterwards at the age of seven-teen transferred to the East India House. This is how he writes of himself when he retired: " It is now six and thirty years since I took my seat in Mincing Lane. Melancholy was the transition at fourteen from the abundant playtime and the frequently intervening vacations of school days, to the eight, nine and sometimes ten hours' a-day attendance at the counting-house. . . . For the first day or two (after my retiral) I felt stunned, overwhelmed. . . . I was in the condition of a prisoner in the old Bastille, suddenly let loose after a forty years' confinement." To boys and girls Lamb is best known for his *Tales from Shakespeare,* which he produced in collaboration with his sister Mary, and *The*

Adventures of Ulysses. His best work, however, is found in his essays which he wrote under the pen-name of Elia. They appeared in the *London Magazine,* and were afterwards published in two volumes *The Essays of Elia* (1823) and *The Last Essays of Elia* (1833). Bridget Elia of the essays is his sister Mary.

ROBERT LYND is a London journalist and literary editor. He was born and educated in Belfast, and began his career as a journalist in Manchester. He has published numerous volumes of essays and sketches.

MARY RUSSELL MITFORD was born at Alresford in Hampshire. She published her first work, a volume of poems, in 1810. She made several attempts as a dramatist, and three of her plays were produced on the stage. But her fame rests on *Our Village,* a series of sketches of English country life and manners, drawn from the village of Three Mile Cross, near Reading, where she lived for a time.

ALEXANDER SMITH was born at Kilmarnock, Ayrshire, where his father was a designer of patterns for lace-work. When the family removed to Glasgow Alexander followed his father's trade for a time until the publication of his first book of poems. In 1854 he was appointed secretary to the University of Edinburgh. In his lifetime he won considerable fame as a poet and journalist, but it is as an essayist that he is now chiefly remembered. His best essays are to be found in the volumes entitled *Dreamthorp, A Summer in Skye* and *Last Leaves.*

ROBERT LOUIS STEVENSON was born in Edinburgh of a famous family of engineers and lighthouse builders. Though he studied for the legal profession and was called to the Scottish Bar, his health made it necessary for him to live an open-air life, and he travelled much in Europe and America. Finally he went to the South Sea island of Samoa, where he died. Stevenson was poet, essayist and novelist, and is best known to boys for *Treasure Island*, *Kidnapped* and *The Black Arrow*, and his poems *Requiem* and *The Vagabond*. *The Trials of a Donkey-Driver* is taken from *Travels with a Donkey in the Cevennes*, an account of a trek or " hike " which he made in the Cevennes mountains.

WILLIAM MAKEPEACE THACKERAY was born in Calcutta where his father was in the service of the East India Company. At the age of five he was sent to England to be educated at Charterhouse and Trinity College, Cambridge. For a time he intended to become an artist and studied art in Paris, but a change in his financial circumstances made it necessary to adopt some profession and he entered journalism. In 1842 he began his contributions to *Punch*. He is, however, best known for his novels, *Vanity Fair*, *Pendennis, The Newcomes, Henry Esmond* and *The Virginians*. His essays, contributed to the *Cornhill Magazine*, were reissued in 1862 as *The Roundabout Papers*.

HENRY DAVID THOREAU was born in the New England state of Massachusetts and educated at Harvard College. He began his career as lecturer and author, but he developed very solitary habits and for a time lived a hermit-like life near Walden Pond. " When I wrote the following pages," he says, " or rather the bulk of them, I lived alone, in the woods, a mile from any neighbour, in a house which I built myself, on the shores of Walden Pond, in Concord, Massachusetts, and earned my living by the labour of my hands only. I lived there two years and two months." " The following pages " refer to *Walden*, a record of his musings on life and his observations of Nature.

INDEX OF AUTHORS